The Billionaire Limit

Jack Donahue

Published by Defenestration Press, 2024.

While every precaution has been taken in the preparation of this book, the publisher assumes no responsibility for errors or omissions, or for damages resulting from the use of the information contained herein.

THE BILLIONAIRE LIMIT

First edition. September 18, 2024.

ISBN: 979-8227839176

Written by Jack Donahue.

Table of Contents

The Billionaire Limit... 1

Chapter 1: The Billionaire Problem................................. 4

Chapter 2: The Ethical Case Against Billionaires.................... 14

Chapter 3: Economic Inefficiency and the Hoarding of Wealth 23

Chapter 4: The Role of Power and Influence............................32

Chapter 5: The Myth of the "Self-Made" Billionaire 40

Chapter 6: The Environmental Cost of Billionaires.................48

Chapter 7: How Billionaires Exploit Workers..........................58

Chapter 8: Wealth Limits: Historical and International Perspectives 68

Chapter 9: Why Philanthropy Isn't the Answer.......................78

Chapter 10: How to Set a Billionaire Limit..............................87

Chapter 11: Redistribution Strategies..................................96

Chapter 12: The Role of Government and Regulation 105

Chapter 13: Social Movements and Grassroots Organizing 116

Chapter 14: Building a Post-Billionaire Economy 127

Chapter 15: The Path Forward 138

Introduction: A World Without Billionaires

In the world we live in today, the existence of billionaires is often seen as an inevitable byproduct of capitalism, or worse, as a sign of its success. Wealth accumulation on such a massive scale is frequently celebrated as a reflection of innovation, hard work, and entrepreneurial genius. Business magazines put billionaires on their covers, books are written about how to emulate their achievements, and governments bend over backward to keep them happy. But what if we told a different story—one that challenges the idea that anyone should ever accumulate a billion-dollar fortune? What if we questioned not just how billionaires are made, but whether billionaires should exist at all?

This book sets out to do exactly that. It challenges the prevailing narrative that extreme wealth is something to be admired or aspired to. It asks readers to consider the moral, economic, and social implications of a world where a handful of people control more wealth than entire nations. In doing so, it invites us to confront some uncomfortable truths about inequality, power, and the structures that allow for such vast disparities of wealth in the first place.

The existence of billionaires is not just a matter of individual success stories. It is a symptom of a system that is deeply imbalanced, where economic growth benefits the few at the expense of the many. When a single person has more wealth than they could ever reasonably use in a lifetime, while millions struggle to afford basic necessities like housing, healthcare, and education, it's clear that something is profoundly wrong.

This book is not simply about decrying billionaires for their wealth. It is about interrogating the systems—economic, political, and cultural—that make such extreme wealth possible. More importantly, it's about exploring what a world without billionaires might look like and how we might get there. It envisions a future where wealth is more equitably distributed, where resources are used to address collective needs rather than personal excess, and where the concentration of wealth no longer threatens the health of our democracies, our economies, and our planet.

The chapters ahead will explore the moral, economic, and environmental costs of billionaires, as well as the policies and actions needed to dismantle the structures that allow extreme wealth accumulation. We will start by examining why billionaires are a problem—not just in theory, but in practice. From there, we'll dive into how wealth at this scale is accumulated, often through exploitation, monopolistic practices, and tax avoidance. We'll consider the influence billionaires wield over politics, media, and public discourse, and the ways in which this influence erodes democracy itself. Along the way, we'll offer concrete proposals for how society can limit extreme wealth, redistribute resources, and move toward a fairer and more just future.

At the heart of this book is a simple but radical proposition: billionaires shouldn't exist. Not because wealth, in and of itself, is inherently bad, but because no one person should have such an outsized share of the world's resources and power. The cost to society, to democracy, and to the planet is simply too great. And it's not enough to rely on the goodwill of billionaires to solve the world's problems through philanthropy or charity. We need systemic change that addresses the root causes of inequality and prevents such extreme concentrations of wealth from accumulating in the first place.

The journey we are about to take together will ask hard questions about fairness, justice, and the kind of world we want to live in. It will challenge us to rethink the assumptions that have shaped our economies and societies for decades. But ultimately, it will offer hope: hope that a more equal and just world is possible, and that a future without billionaires can be one where prosperity and dignity are shared by all, not hoarded by a few.

Let's imagine a world without billionaires. And let's get to work on building it.

Chapter 1: The Billionaire Problem

The existence of billionaires represents one of the most extreme forms of wealth inequality in human history. At the core of this issue is the growing concentration of wealth in the hands of a tiny elite while the vast majority of people struggle with economic instability, stagnant wages, and a diminishing quality of life. This chapter explores the moral, economic, and social issues surrounding billionaires, explaining how their wealth distorts societies and weakens democratic systems. Moreover, it will highlight how this extreme concentration of wealth exacerbates global problems like inequality, environmental degradation, and the erosion of public services.

The Scale of Wealth Disparity

To understand the magnitude of the billionaire problem, one must first grasp the scale of wealth disparity in today's world. As of recent estimates, the combined wealth of the world's richest 2,000 billionaires exceeds several trillion dollars. Meanwhile, millions of people live in poverty, lacking access to basic necessities like clean water, healthcare, and education. In countries like the United States, this wealth gap is particularly pronounced, where the top 1% controls more wealth than the bottom 90% combined.

The sheer volume of wealth owned by a select few individuals is staggering. For example, in 2021, the richest man in the world had a net worth exceeding $200 billion, a sum so vast that it is difficult to conceptualize. To put this into perspective, a person spending $10,000 every day would take more than 27,000 years to spend just one billion dollars. The absurdity of such fortunes becomes more apparent when compared to the struggles of billions of people who live on less than $5.50 a day. This stark contrast exposes the problem at the heart of the billionaire phenomenon: the vast disparity in resources is neither necessary nor justified in a world where so many are deprived of basic human rights.

Wealth, when concentrated in the hands of a few, does not simply reflect the success of those individuals; it reflects a broader societal failure to distribute resources equitably. This failure has significant consequences for everyone, not just those left behind by extreme inequality. As inequality grows, so too do the social and economic problems that stem from it, weakening societies and undermining long-term prosperity.

The Morality of Extreme Wealth

The existence of billionaires raises fundamental questions about fairness and justice in modern society. From a moral perspective, extreme wealth is difficult to justify when billions of people face deprivation and hardship. The idea that any single individual can accumulate more wealth than they could ever reasonably need, while others struggle to survive, flies in the face of basic ethical principles of equity and human dignity.

Wealth inequality also creates a significant moral dilemma because it contradicts the notion of equal opportunity. Billionaires often argue that they earned their fortunes through hard work, innovation, or entrepreneurship. However, this narrative obscures the reality that many billionaires are born into privilege and benefit from inherited wealth, favorable social conditions, and an economic system designed to perpetuate their dominance. Even those who build their wealth from modest beginnings rely on public infrastructures, taxpayer-funded education systems, and the labor of others to achieve their success.

When we examine the systemic advantages that billionaires enjoy, it becomes clear that extreme wealth is often the result of structural inequities, not just individual merit. The ethical question then becomes: Is it right for a few to accumulate vast fortunes by exploiting systems that are meant to serve everyone, especially when those fortunes come at the expense of the broader public? This leads to the conclusion that extreme wealth is not merely an issue of personal success, but one of societal failure, where the systems designed to ensure the well-being of all are instead rigged to benefit a tiny elite.

Economic Consequences of Billionaire Wealth

The economic problems stemming from billionaire wealth are profound and far-reaching. When wealth becomes concentrated in the hands of a few, it distorts the economy in ways that hinder growth, innovation, and broad-based prosperity. Billionaires often accumulate wealth through monopolistic practices, stock buybacks, and other mechanisms that prioritize short-term profits over long-term investment in the real economy. This behavior creates an economic landscape where corporate power dominates, competition is stifled, and innovation is limited.

One of the most visible effects of concentrated wealth is the stagnation of wages for ordinary workers. Over the past few decades, worker productivity has increased significantly, yet wages have remained largely stagnant or even declined in real terms. At the same time, executive pay and shareholder profits have skyrocketed. Billionaires, as the owners and executives of major corporations, are often the primary beneficiaries of these economic dynamics. Their wealth grows exponentially, while the wages of the workers who drive their businesses remain stagnant. This creates a situation where wealth accumulates at the top, further deepening inequality.

In addition to wage stagnation, billionaire wealth distorts markets in ways that make it harder for small businesses and entrepreneurs to succeed. Through their control of large corporations, billionaires can use their economic power to crush competition, buy out rivals, and maintain monopolies or oligopolies. This limits consumer choice, drives up prices, and concentrates even more power and wealth in the hands of the few. In sectors like technology, media, and retail, the dominance of billionaire-owned corporations has created environments where it is increasingly difficult for new entrants to challenge the status quo.

Furthermore, the accumulation of wealth by billionaires often leads to speculative investments and financialization of the economy, where money is directed toward financial markets rather than productive industries. This can result in economic bubbles, such as the housing market crash of 2008, where speculative behavior fueled by vast sums of wealth creates instability and crises that disproportionately affect the middle and lower classes. When the financial system collapses, it is often everyday people who bear the brunt of the consequences, while billionaires and corporations receive government bailouts and other forms of financial support.

The Impact on Democracy

The billionaire problem is not just an economic issue; it is a political one as well. The concentration of wealth in the hands of a few leads to an outsized influence on political systems, undermining democratic principles and eroding public trust in government. Billionaires use their wealth to shape policy in ways that benefit their interests, often at the expense of the broader public. This can take many forms, from campaign donations and lobbying efforts to the control of media outlets and the funding of think tanks and advocacy groups.

One of the most significant ways billionaires influence politics is through their ability to finance political campaigns. In many countries, political campaigns require vast sums of money to be competitive, and billionaires are able to provide that funding. As a result, politicians often become beholden to the interests of their wealthy donors rather than the needs of their constituents. This creates a situation where the policies that are enacted reflect the desires of the wealthy elite, rather than the will of the people. Issues like tax reform, labor rights, healthcare, and environmental regulation are often shaped by the interests of billionaires who stand to benefit from maintaining the status quo.

Lobbying is another tool that billionaires use to influence political outcomes. Through their control of corporations, billionaires can deploy armies of lobbyists to shape legislation and regulation in ways that protect their wealth and power. For example, billionaires in industries like finance, energy, and pharmaceuticals have been able to weaken regulations that protect consumers and the environment, ensuring that their profits remain untouched by government intervention. This level of influence erodes the ability of governments to act in the public interest and further cements the power of the wealthy elite.

Billionaire-owned media outlets also play a significant role in shaping public opinion and political discourse. By controlling major news networks, newspapers, and digital platforms, billionaires can influence the way information is presented to the public, framing issues in ways that support their interests. This control over the media limits the diversity of viewpoints and reduces the ability of ordinary citizens to make informed decisions about political matters. When the media becomes concentrated in the hands of a few wealthy individuals, democracy suffers because the public's access to unbiased information is compromised.

The Exploitation of Labor and Public Resources

Billionaire wealth often accumulates through systems that exploit labor and public resources. This is perhaps the most significant aspect of the billionaire problem: extreme wealth is rarely generated in isolation; it relies on the exploitation of others. Billionaires typically owe their fortunes to the labor of thousands, if not millions, of workers who receive a fraction of the wealth they create. Moreover, many billionaires amass their fortunes by taking advantage of public resources and infrastructure, using taxpayer-funded systems to generate private profits.

One of the most glaring examples of this exploitation can be seen in the low wages and poor working conditions that many billionaires' businesses impose on their employees. From retail workers in global supply chains to factory workers in developing countries, the people who produce the goods and services that make billionaires rich often work in conditions that are unsafe, underpaid, and devoid of basic labor protections. This is particularly true in industries like fast fashion, tech manufacturing, and e-commerce, where the drive for profit maximization leads to the squeezing of labor costs at every turn.

The rise of the gig economy has only exacerbated this problem. Platforms like Uber, Lyft, and DoorDash, which have made their founders and investors into billionaires, rely on a model that treats workers as independent contractors rather than employees. This allows these companies to avoid providing basic benefits like healthcare, retirement contributions, and paid time off, while still profiting from the labor of millions of drivers and delivery workers. The result is a new class of precarious workers who are essential to the business models of billionaire-owned companies but are denied the protections and rights that traditional employees enjoy.

In addition to exploiting labor, billionaires often accumulate wealth by using public resources and infrastructure without adequately compensating society. For instance, tech billionaires rely on publicly funded research and development in areas like the internet, artificial intelligence, and biotechnology, yet the profits from these innovations are captured by private companies rather than being shared with the public. Similarly, billionaires in industries like real estate and natural resources often benefit from favorable government policies, subsidies, and access to public lands, all of which are funded by taxpayers.

This pattern of exploiting public resources for private gain is particularly evident in the case of corporate tax avoidance. Many billionaires and their companies use complex legal strategies to minimize their tax burdens, often paying far less in taxes than the average worker. This deprives governments of the revenue needed to fund public services like healthcare, education, and infrastructure, while allowing billionaires to accumulate even more wealth. In essence, the public is subsidizing the lifestyles of the ultra-wealthy by shouldering the burden of providing the resources and systems that billionaires rely on to generate their fortunes.

The Global Impact of Billionaire Wealth

The billionaire problem is not confined to any one country; it is a global issue that affects societies around the world. In developing countries, the existence of billionaires can exacerbate existing inequalities and undermine efforts to promote sustainable development. Many billionaires in these countries accumulate wealth by exploiting natural resources, underpaying workers, and engaging in corrupt practices that weaken governance and erode the rule of law.

In countries with weak regulatory systems, billionaires often operate with impunity, using their wealth to influence governments and avoid accountability. This creates a situation where the rich get richer, while the poor are left to deal with the environmental degradation, economic instability, and political corruption that billionaire wealth generates. The global nature of the billionaire problem also means that solutions must be international in scope, requiring cooperation between governments, institutions, and civil society to address the root causes of wealth inequality.

The existence of billionaires is not just a byproduct of economic success; it is a symptom of a deeply flawed system that allows extreme wealth to accumulate in the hands of a few at the expense of the many. This concentration of wealth creates profound moral, economic, and political problems that weaken societies and undermine democracy. Billionaire wealth is often built on the exploitation of labor, the misuse of public resources, and the manipulation of political systems, all of which contribute to the growing inequality that plagues modern economies.

As we will explore in the chapters that follow, addressing the billionaire problem requires a fundamental rethinking of how wealth is distributed and how economic systems are structured. Limiting extreme wealth and redistributing resources more equitably is not only a matter of fairness but also a necessity for building a more just, sustainable, and democratic world.

Chapter 2: The Ethical Case Against Billionaires

The existence of billionaires raises fundamental ethical questions about fairness, justice, and the moral obligations of individuals and society. Can we justify a system where a tiny fraction of humanity controls more wealth than entire nations, while billions of people struggle to meet basic needs like food, healthcare, and education? The ethical critique of billionaires is not simply about their wealth itself, but about the broader consequences of extreme wealth inequality. This chapter explores these issues through various ethical lenses, drawing on principles of fairness, social justice, and human rights to argue that the accumulation of vast fortunes by a few is morally indefensible. It contrasts the lives of billionaires with the harsh realities of global poverty, poor healthcare access, and unequal educational opportunities, suggesting that such disparities undermine the moral fabric of society.

Wealth Inequality as an Ethical Problem

At its core, the ethical case against billionaires stems from the problem of extreme wealth inequality. Wealth inequality is not just an economic issue; it is an ethical one that speaks to the kind of society we want to live in and the values we hold as human beings. The central question is whether it is morally acceptable for a few individuals to hold such disproportionate wealth while so many others live in deprivation.

Fairness and the Distribution of Wealth

THE BILLIONAIRE LIMIT

One of the most prominent ethical principles at play in discussions of wealth inequality is fairness. Fairness is a foundational concept in moral philosophy, often linked to the idea that individuals should have equal opportunities to succeed and thrive. However, in a world where billionaires exist, fairness is called into question because the playing field is anything but level.

The concept of fairness demands that people have access to the same opportunities, that they are not unduly disadvantaged by circumstances beyond their control, such as the family they are born into, their access to education, or their geographic location. Yet, the vast fortunes of billionaires often reflect the opposite: the deep entrenchment of privilege and the perpetuation of systemic inequalities. Many billionaires inherit their wealth, and even those who do not often benefit from social, educational, and economic advantages that are unavailable to most people.

Take, for example, a child born into a billionaire family versus a child born into poverty. The billionaire's child will likely receive the best education money can buy, have access to influential social networks, and inherit significant financial resources. On the other hand, the child born into poverty may struggle to access quality education, healthcare, and even basic nutrition. The fairness of the system is immediately compromised when such stark disparities exist from birth, and the opportunity for upward mobility is limited for the vast majority.

Even for those who argue that hard work and innovation should be rewarded, the question arises: How much wealth is fair? Is there a point at which the accumulation of wealth becomes excessive, even if it is earned through hard work or innovation? Ethical considerations suggest that there must be a limit, especially when vast fortunes come at the expense of others who are struggling to meet their basic needs.

Social Justice and the Common Good

Another key ethical framework for examining the billionaire phenomenon is the principle of social justice. Social justice is concerned with ensuring that all members of society have their basic needs met and that resources are distributed in a way that promotes the well-being of the collective. In a just society, wealth and resources should be allocated in ways that prioritize the common good over individual accumulation.

Billionaires, by definition, represent an extreme deviation from the idea of social justice. When one person accumulates more wealth than they could possibly need or spend in a lifetime, while others lack access to housing, food, or healthcare, the distribution of resources is fundamentally unjust. The common good is undermined when so much wealth is concentrated in the hands of a few, leaving the rest of society to grapple with the consequences of poverty, poor healthcare, and inadequate public services.

Social justice also calls into question the way that billionaire wealth is often acquired. Many billionaires accumulate their fortunes by taking advantage of systems that prioritize profits over people, such as underpaying workers, exploiting natural resources, or benefiting from lax tax policies that allow them to avoid contributing their fair share to the public good. In these cases, billionaire wealth is not simply the result of individual effort or innovation, but of systemic exploitation that perpetuates inequality and injustice.

Human Rights and Global Poverty

A critical ethical issue related to billionaires is the impact of extreme wealth on global poverty and human rights. The United Nations' Universal Declaration of Human Rights outlines basic human rights to which every person is entitled, including the right to adequate food, clothing, housing, medical care, education, and social services. Yet, in a world where billionaires exist, billions of people are denied these basic rights.

Consider the global issue of poverty. According to the World Bank, nearly 700 million people live in extreme poverty, surviving on less than $1.90 a day. In contrast, billionaires possess fortunes so vast that they could end extreme poverty many times over. For example, estimates suggest that the wealth of the world's richest individuals could easily fund universal access to basic education, healthcare, and clean water for all. The ethical question here is clear: Is it morally acceptable for a small group of individuals to hold such immense wealth when so many people are denied their basic human rights?

Billionaire wealth, therefore, represents not just an inequality in resources but an inequality in human dignity. While billions of people suffer from hunger, lack of healthcare, and inadequate education, billionaires enjoy lives of luxury and excess. This disparity undermines the fundamental principle that every human being deserves a life of dignity and opportunity. It is not merely a failure of the economic system but a profound moral failure of society to allow such disparities to persist.

The Utilitarian Argument: The Greatest Good for the Greatest Number

Utilitarianism is an ethical theory that suggests that the right course of action is the one that maximizes happiness and well-being for the greatest number of people. Under this framework, billionaire wealth is ethically problematic because it fails to maximize the well-being of society as a whole. Instead, it concentrates resources in the hands of a few individuals, often at the expense of the many.

Consider how wealth could be distributed more equitably to benefit a larger portion of society. The money tied up in billionaires' fortunes could be used to fund social programs, healthcare, education, and infrastructure projects that would improve the lives of millions, if not billions, of people. From a utilitarian perspective, this would result in a far greater sum of well-being than allowing a few individuals to retain their vast fortunes for personal use.

Take healthcare as an example. In the United States, millions of people are uninsured or underinsured, unable to afford basic medical care. Meanwhile, the country's billionaires could easily fund universal healthcare coverage, providing life-saving treatments and preventive care for millions. The same argument applies to education: Many of the world's billionaires could single-handedly fund universal access to primary and secondary education, helping to break the cycle of poverty for countless individuals. From a utilitarian perspective, redirecting billionaire wealth toward these social goods would result in a far greater benefit to society than allowing billionaires to continue accumulating vast sums of money.

The Limits of Personal Use and Excessive Wealth

One of the most striking ethical issues related to billionaires is the sheer excess of their wealth relative to what is necessary for personal use. There is a limit to how much wealth any individual can reasonably use in a lifetime, and yet billionaires continue to accumulate more and more. This raises the question: What is the purpose of such excessive wealth, and is it morally justifiable to hoard resources that could otherwise be used to improve the lives of millions?

Consider the lifestyles of billionaires, many of whom own multiple mansions, private jets, yachts, and other symbols of extreme luxury. While some argue that billionaires should be free to spend their money as they choose, the ethical issue lies in the contrast between their extravagance and the widespread suffering that persists around the world. The moral philosopher Peter Singer has famously argued that if we have the means to alleviate suffering, we have a moral obligation to do so. Under this framework, it becomes difficult to justify the continued accumulation of wealth by billionaires when that wealth could be used to alleviate poverty, treat preventable diseases, and improve living conditions for millions of people.

Even for billionaires who engage in philanthropy, there are ethical concerns about the control they exercise over how their wealth is used. Philanthropy is often presented as a solution to the problems caused by extreme wealth, but it can also serve to reinforce the power and influence of billionaires. Instead of allowing democratically elected governments to decide how resources should be allocated for the public good, philanthropy places this power in the hands of a few wealthy individuals. This undermines the principle of democratic accountability and raises ethical questions about the role of billionaires in shaping public policy and social outcomes.

The Role of Luck and Structural Inequality

Another ethical argument against billionaires is the role that luck and structural inequality play in the accumulation of wealth. While billionaires often attribute their success to hard work, intelligence, or innovation, the reality is that luck and systemic advantages play a significant role in determining who becomes wealthy and who does not. Factors such as being born into a wealthy family, having access to elite education, and benefiting from favorable economic and political conditions all contribute to the accumulation of wealth.

The philosopher John Rawls argued that a just society is one in which inequalities are only permissible if they benefit the least advantaged members of society. Under this framework, extreme wealth inequality, as exemplified by billionaires, is ethically problematic because it fails to meet this criterion. Instead, billionaires often amass their wealth through systems that perpetuate inequality, such as underpaying workers, exploiting natural resources, and avoiding taxes. These systems create a situation where the wealthy become wealthier, while the poor are left with fewer opportunities to improve their circumstances.

Furthermore, the concept of "meritocracy" is often used to justify the existence of billionaires, suggesting that those who work the hardest or are the most talented deserve to be rewarded with vast wealth. However, this notion ignores the structural inequalities that limit opportunities for most people. In reality, many of the world's poorest individuals work long hours in difficult conditions, yet they remain trapped in poverty because of systemic barriers that prevent them from advancing. The existence of billionaires, therefore, reflects not a meritocratic system but a deeply unequal one that rewards privilege and perpetuates injustice.

The ethical case against billionaires is compelling and multifaceted. From the principles of fairness and social justice to the recognition of human rights and the limits of personal use, the accumulation of vast wealth by a few individuals raises profound moral concerns. In a world where billions of people lack access to basic necessities, the existence of billionaires represents not only an economic failure but a moral one as well.

Billionaire wealth is often built on systems of exploitation and inequality, and its concentration in the hands of a few undermines the common good and perpetuates injustice.

Addressing the ethical problems posed by billionaires requires not only a rethinking of our economic systems but also a renewed commitment to the values of fairness, social justice, and human dignity. In the chapters that follow, we will explore how society can move toward a more equitable distribution of wealth and resources, creating a world where the well-being of the many is prioritized over the accumulation of wealth by the few.

Chapter 3: Economic Inefficiency and the Hoarding of Wealth

The existence of billionaires is not only an ethical and social issue but also a significant economic problem. The extreme concentration of wealth among a small group of individuals creates distortions within the economy, leading to inefficiencies that stifle broader growth and hinder innovation. While defenders of billionaires often argue that their wealth stimulates investment, job creation, and economic growth, the reality is that much of this wealth is hoarded in ways that benefit a select few, rather than contributing to the well-being of society as a whole.

This chapter explores the economic implications of extreme wealth concentration, arguing that billionaires hoard wealth in ways that distort markets, reduce economic dynamism, and prevent wealth from being distributed more efficiently. By concentrating resources in the hands of a few, billionaires limit the potential for broader economic growth and reduce the ability of ordinary people to participate fully in the economy. In contrast, redistributing this wealth could stimulate demand, promote job creation, and foster a more vibrant and innovative economy.

The Economic Distortion of Wealth Concentration

One of the primary arguments against the existence of billionaires is that they distort the natural functioning of the economy by concentrating wealth and resources in ways that are inefficient and harmful to long-term economic health. In an ideal economy, wealth would circulate freely, with individuals spending money on goods and services, businesses investing in productive ventures, and governments funding essential public services. However, when a small group of individuals accumulates vast amounts of wealth, this circulation is disrupted, leading to a situation where resources are hoarded rather than used to stimulate economic growth.

Billionaires often hoard wealth in financial assets, such as stocks, bonds, real estate, or other forms of capital that do not directly contribute to economic activity. While some of these investments may yield returns for the billionaire, they do little to promote job creation or innovation in the broader economy. Instead, the wealth remains concentrated in financial markets, benefiting a small group of investors while leaving the rest of society to struggle with stagnating wages, rising inequality, and reduced economic mobility.

This concentration of wealth also skews the allocation of resources within the economy. For example, billionaires are more likely to invest in low-risk, high-return ventures that serve their own interests, such as real estate speculation, stock buybacks, or other financial instruments that do not necessarily contribute to long-term economic growth. These types of investments do little to create new jobs, promote technological innovation, or address pressing social challenges. Instead, they exacerbate existing inequalities by increasing the value of assets that are already owned by the wealthy, while leaving ordinary workers and consumers behind.

The Hoarding of Wealth and Its Impact on Economic Growth

The problem of hoarding wealth by billionaires goes beyond simple inequality; it creates significant inefficiencies in how the economy functions. In a healthy economy, money is spent, invested, and circulated, leading to increased demand for goods and services, more job creation, and greater overall economic growth. However, when wealth is hoarded by billionaires, this cycle is interrupted, as vast sums of money are taken out of circulation and parked in unproductive assets.

One of the key ways in which wealth hoarding impacts the economy is by reducing aggregate demand. Aggregate demand refers to the total demand for goods and services in the economy, which is a key driver of economic growth. When billionaires hoard wealth, they are not spending it on goods and services in the same way that ordinary consumers would. Instead, much of this wealth is stored in financial markets or invested in luxury assets, which do little to stimulate broader demand.

This reduction in aggregate demand has significant consequences for the economy as a whole. When demand for goods and services is low, businesses have less incentive to invest in new production, expand their operations, or hire additional workers. As a result, job creation slows, wages stagnate, and economic growth becomes sluggish. This creates a vicious cycle, where reduced demand leads to slower growth, which in turn leads to further reductions in demand as workers and consumers have less money to spend.

In contrast, redistributing wealth from billionaires to ordinary consumers could have a dramatic impact on aggregate demand and economic growth. When wealth is more evenly distributed, ordinary people are more likely to spend it on goods and services, which creates a multiplier effect throughout the economy. For example, a middle-class family that receives a tax cut or a wage increase is more likely to spend that money on housing, education, healthcare, or other essential goods and services. This increased demand, in turn, stimulates businesses to invest in new production, hire more workers, and innovate to meet consumer needs.

Investment and Innovation: Billionaires vs. Society

One of the arguments often made in defense of billionaires is that they are essential for promoting investment and innovation. Proponents of this view argue that billionaires, through their wealth and business acumen, have the ability to fund new ventures, invest in cutting-edge technologies, and create jobs that benefit society as a whole. However, this argument overlooks the fact that much of billionaire wealth is invested in ways that do not contribute to meaningful innovation or job creation. Instead, it is often invested in self-serving ventures that reinforce existing wealth and privilege.

A significant portion of billionaire wealth is tied up in speculative investments, such as real estate development, financial markets, or other forms of capital accumulation that do little to promote long-term economic growth or innovation. For example, real estate speculation by billionaires can drive up housing prices, making it more difficult for ordinary people to afford homes. Similarly, stock buybacks—where companies purchase their own shares to drive up stock prices—benefit wealthy investors but do little to create jobs or improve productivity.

Moreover, billionaires are more likely to invest in ventures that offer high returns with minimal risk, rather than funding truly transformative innovations that could benefit society as a whole. This tendency toward risk aversion is a result of the fact that billionaires have so much to lose. When individuals or institutions accumulate vast amounts of wealth, they often become more cautious in their investment strategies, preferring to preserve their wealth rather than take risks that could lead to significant losses.

In contrast, if wealth were distributed more broadly, there would be more opportunities for individuals and businesses to take risks, innovate, and create new industries. Small and medium-sized businesses, which are often the engines of innovation and job creation, would have greater access to capital, allowing them to experiment with new ideas and technologies. Moreover, when wealth is more evenly distributed, ordinary people have more financial security, which allows them to take risks, such as starting new businesses or pursuing further education.

The Myth of the Job-Creating Billionaire

Another common defense of billionaires is the idea that they are "job creators" who drive economic growth by investing in businesses and creating employment opportunities. However, this argument is largely a myth. While some billionaires do create jobs through their businesses, the overall impact of billionaire wealth on job creation is far smaller than it is often portrayed.

In reality, most jobs are created by small and medium-sized businesses, not by billionaires or large corporations. According to the U.S. Small Business Administration, small businesses account for nearly half of all private-sector employment and are responsible for the majority of new job creation. These businesses often operate on thin margins and rely on consumer spending to stay afloat. When wealth is concentrated in the hands of billionaires, ordinary consumers have less money to spend, which reduces demand for goods and services and hampers the ability of small businesses to grow and create jobs.

Moreover, many billionaires accumulate their wealth by cutting jobs, reducing wages, and automating work. For example, large corporations often engage in practices such as outsourcing, offshoring, and downsizing in order to maximize profits. While these strategies may benefit shareholders and boost the personal wealth of billionaires, they often come at the expense of workers and the broader economy. As jobs are eliminated and wages are suppressed, workers have less money to spend, which reduces overall demand and slows economic growth.

In contrast, redistributing wealth from billionaires to ordinary workers could have a far greater impact on job creation. When workers have higher wages and more financial security, they are more likely to spend money on goods and services, which creates demand for businesses and leads to job growth. Additionally, redistributing wealth to fund public investments in infrastructure, education, and healthcare could create millions of new jobs, while also improving the quality of life for ordinary people.

The Role of Tax Policy in Wealth Hoarding

Tax policy plays a crucial role in the economic inefficiencies created by billionaire wealth. Over the past several decades, tax policies in many countries have shifted in ways that benefit the wealthy at the expense of the broader population. In particular, lower taxes on capital gains, inheritance, and corporate profits have allowed billionaires to accumulate vast fortunes without contributing their fair share to the public good.

One of the key mechanisms through which billionaires hoard wealth is by taking advantage of favorable tax treatment for investments in capital assets, such as stocks, bonds, and real estate. In many countries, capital gains are taxed at lower rates than income earned through labor, which disproportionately benefits the wealthy. This tax advantage encourages billionaires to invest in financial markets, where they can earn high returns with minimal tax liability, rather than investing in productive ventures that create jobs and stimulate economic growth.

Similarly, inheritance tax policies in many countries allow billionaire wealth to be passed down to future generations with minimal taxation. This perpetuates wealth inequality by ensuring that billionaire families maintain their fortunes, while ordinary families are left to struggle with rising costs of living and stagnant wages. The result is a system where wealth becomes increasingly concentrated in the hands of a few, while the broader economy suffers from reduced demand and lower economic mobility.

The Benefits of Redistributing Wealth

Redistributing wealth from billionaires to the broader population could have significant economic benefits, both in terms of stimulating demand and promoting long-term growth. One of the most effective ways to do this is through progressive taxation, which ensures that the wealthiest individuals contribute their fair share to the public good.

A progressive tax system, where tax rates increase with income and wealth, could help to reduce the concentration of wealth among billionaires, while also funding essential public investments in healthcare, education, and infrastructure. These investments would create jobs, stimulate demand, and improve the overall quality of life for ordinary people. Moreover, by reducing the tax advantages enjoyed by billionaires, governments could encourage more productive investments in innovation, job creation, and social well-being.

In addition to progressive taxation, other policies such as universal basic income, stronger labor protections, and increased public investment in social services could help to redistribute wealth more equitably. Universal basic income, for example, would provide every individual with a guaranteed income, ensuring that everyone has access to basic necessities and can participate fully in the economy. This would not only reduce poverty but also stimulate demand by giving ordinary people more money to spend on goods and services.

The economic inefficiencies created by billionaires are significant and far-reaching. By hoarding wealth in unproductive assets, concentrating resources in the hands of a few, and reducing aggregate demand, billionaires distort the natural functioning of the economy and hinder long-term growth. The myth that billionaires are essential for job creation and innovation is largely unfounded, as most jobs are created by small and medium-sized businesses, and much of billionaire wealth is invested in self-serving ventures that do little to benefit society.

Redistributing wealth from billionaires to the broader population could have profound economic benefits, including increased demand, greater job creation, and a more vibrant and innovative economy. By implementing policies such as progressive taxation, universal basic income, and public investment in social services, governments can help to reduce wealth inequality and create a more efficient and equitable economic system. In the chapters that follow, we will explore specific policy proposals and strategies for addressing the economic and social problems caused by extreme wealth concentration, and how we can build a more just and prosperous society for all.

Chapter 4: The Role of Power and Influence

The existence of billionaires doesn't just skew the economic landscape—it also profoundly distorts political and social systems. In democratic societies, the ideal is that every individual has an equal voice in shaping the laws and policies that govern their lives. However, when wealth becomes concentrated in the hands of a few, the reality is that these individuals gain outsized power and influence over political institutions, media narratives, and social norms. This chapter delves into the relationship between concentrated wealth and political power, demonstrating how billionaires use their fortunes to shape elections, influence policy, and control public discourse.

By doing so, billionaires undermine the foundations of democracy, making it increasingly difficult for ordinary citizens to have their voices heard and their needs addressed. Instead, public policy often becomes skewed toward the interests of the wealthy, exacerbating inequality and further marginalizing vulnerable populations. This chapter explores the various mechanisms through which billionaires exert influence, including political donations, lobbying, media ownership, and social initiatives. Through these mechanisms, they are able to entrench their wealth and power, making it harder for democratic processes to function as intended.

Billionaires and Political Donations

THE BILLIONAIRE LIMIT

One of the most direct ways in which billionaires influence the political system is through campaign donations. In many democratic societies, political campaigns are incredibly expensive, and candidates rely heavily on wealthy donors to finance their bids for office. Billionaires, with their vast resources, are able to contribute far more than ordinary citizens, giving them a disproportionate voice in determining which candidates have the financial backing needed to succeed.

In the United States, for example, the Citizens United decision of 2010 significantly expanded the influence of wealthy individuals in politics by allowing unlimited contributions to political action committees (PACs) and super PACs. These organizations can spend unlimited amounts of money to support or oppose candidates, as long as they do not coordinate directly with the campaigns. As a result, billionaires can effectively bankroll entire political campaigns, ensuring that candidates who align with their interests have a significant financial advantage over their opponents.

The influence of billionaires on political campaigns isn't limited to direct contributions. Many billionaires also fund think tanks, advocacy groups, and policy organizations that shape the political landscape. These organizations produce research, lobby lawmakers, and run public campaigns to influence policy debates in ways that align with the interests of the wealthy. For example, billionaires like the Koch brothers have used their wealth to fund a network of libertarian organizations that promote policies such as deregulation, tax cuts for the wealthy, and opposition to environmental regulations.

In many cases, the policies advocated by billionaire-backed organizations directly benefit the wealthy while harming ordinary citizens. For example, tax cuts for the rich may reduce government revenues, leading to cuts in public services that disproportionately affect low- and middle-income families. Similarly, deregulation of industries may lead to environmental degradation, unsafe working conditions, or financial instability, all of which have a greater impact on the most vulnerable members of society.

Lobbying and Policy Influence

In addition to campaign donations, billionaires exert influence through lobbying efforts. Lobbying involves direct interaction with lawmakers and government officials to shape legislation and policy decisions. While lobbying is a common practice in many industries, billionaires have a unique advantage due to their ability to fund extensive lobbying operations that far outmatch those of ordinary citizens or small advocacy groups.

In the United States, lobbying is a multibillion-dollar industry, and billionaires often fund lobbyists who advocate for policies that serve their interests. For example, wealthy individuals and corporations frequently lobby for lower taxes, fewer regulations, and favorable trade policies. These efforts often result in legislation that benefits the wealthy while undermining protections for workers, consumers, and the environment.

A prime example of billionaire influence through lobbying is the role of the pharmaceutical industry in shaping U.S.

healthcare policy. Pharmaceutical companies, many of which are owned or controlled by billionaires, spend hundreds of millions of dollars each year on lobbying efforts. These efforts have successfully blocked legislation that would allow Medicare to negotiate drug prices, resulting in higher prescription drug costs for ordinary Americans. At the same time, pharmaceutical companies have pushed for patent protections that prevent generic competitors from entering the market, ensuring that they can maintain monopoly pricing on essential medications.

In addition to healthcare, billionaires exert influence in a wide range of policy areas, including climate change, labor laws, and financial regulations. In many cases, the policies they advocate for are designed to protect their wealth and power, even if they come at the expense of the broader public. For example, many billionaires have opposed efforts to raise the minimum wage, arguing that it would harm businesses and reduce job creation. However, research has shown that raising the minimum wage would lift millions of workers out of poverty and stimulate economic growth by increasing consumer spending.

The ability of billionaires to shape policy through lobbying creates a feedback loop in which their wealth allows them to influence the political system, and the policies they advocate for further entrench their wealth and power. This cycle makes it increasingly difficult for ordinary citizens to have their voices heard in the political process, as the interests of the wealthy take precedence over the needs of the broader population.

Media Ownership and Control

Beyond direct political influence, billionaires also shape public discourse through their control of the media. In many countries, media ownership is concentrated in the hands of a few wealthy individuals, giving them significant power over what information is disseminated to the public and how it is framed. This concentration of media ownership has profound implications for democracy, as it allows billionaires to shape public opinion in ways that serve their interests.

For example, in the United States, media mogul Rupert Murdoch, whose net worth is estimated to be in the billions, owns a significant portion of the country's media landscape, including Fox News, The Wall Street Journal, and The New York Post. Through these outlets, Murdoch has been able to promote conservative viewpoints and shape public discourse on issues such as immigration, healthcare, and climate change. Fox News, in particular, has been criticized for promoting misinformation and partisan narratives that align with the interests of wealthy individuals and corporations.

Similarly, in other countries, billionaires have used their control of the media to influence political outcomes. In Italy, for example, billionaire Silvio Berlusconi used his media empire to promote his political career and shape public opinion in his favor. Berlusconi's control of Italy's largest private television network, Mediaset, allowed him to dominate the airwaves and influence the outcome of elections, ensuring that his political party remained in power for much of the 1990s and 2000s.

The concentration of media ownership in the hands of billionaires creates a situation in which a small number of individuals have disproportionate control over the information that reaches the public. This undermines the democratic principle of a free and independent press, as media outlets become more concerned with serving the interests of their owners than with providing objective and accurate reporting. In some cases, this has led to the suppression of important stories or the promotion of misleading narratives that protect the wealth and power of billionaires.

Shaping Social and Cultural Norms

In addition to influencing politics and media, billionaires also play a significant role in shaping social and cultural norms. Through philanthropy, business ventures, and social initiatives, billionaires are able to promote their own vision of what society should look like. While some of these initiatives may be well-intentioned, they often serve to reinforce the power and privilege of the wealthy, rather than addressing the root causes of inequality.

One of the ways in which billionaires shape social norms is through their philanthropic efforts. Many billionaires donate large sums of money to charitable causes, such as education, healthcare, and environmental conservation. While these donations may appear to be altruistic, they often come with strings attached. Billionaires who fund charitable organizations or public institutions, such as universities, often exert influence over the direction of these organizations, shaping their priorities and policies in ways that align with the donor's interests.

For example, billionaire philanthropist Bill Gates has been heavily involved in shaping global health policy through his foundation, the Bill & Melinda Gates Foundation. While the foundation has funded important initiatives, such as efforts to combat infectious diseases and improve access to healthcare, critics have raised concerns about the foundation's influence over global health priorities. Some argue that the Gates Foundation's focus on technological solutions, such as vaccines and pharmaceutical treatments, has led to an underinvestment in more systemic solutions, such as strengthening public health systems and addressing the social determinants of health.

Similarly, billionaires often use their philanthropic efforts to influence education policy. In the United States, several billionaires, including Gates, have funded initiatives to promote charter schools and education reform. While these efforts are often framed as a way to improve educational outcomes for disadvantaged students, critics argue that they undermine public education by diverting resources away from traditional public schools and promoting a market-based approach to education that benefits private interests.

Philanthropy, while often presented as a way for billionaires to give back to society, can also serve as a form of reputation management, allowing wealthy individuals to deflect criticism of their business practices while maintaining control over how their wealth is used. This can create a situation in which billionaires are able to dictate the terms of social progress, rather than allowing democratic processes to determine how resources are allocated and what social issues are prioritized.

The Erosion of Democratic Principles

The concentration of wealth and power in the hands of billionaires poses a serious threat to democratic principles. In a democracy, the ideal is that all citizens have an equal say in shaping the laws and policies that govern their lives. However, when a small group of individuals is able to exert disproportionate influence over political institutions, media narratives, and social norms, this ideal is undermined.

Billionaire influence erodes democracy in several ways. First, it skews the political process in favor of the wealthy, as billionaires are able to use their financial resources to support candidates and policies that align with their interests. This reduces the ability of ordinary citizens to have their voices heard and

their needs addressed. Second, billionaire control of the media allows them to shape public opinion in ways that protect their wealth and power, further distorting the democratic process. Finally, through their philanthropic efforts and social initiatives, billionaires are able to promote their own vision of what society should look like, often at the expense of more democratic and inclusive approaches to social progress.

Chapter 5: The Myth of the "Self-Made" Billionaire

The concept of the "self-made billionaire" is one of the most enduring myths in modern capitalist society. According to this narrative, individuals who reach billionaire status have done so through sheer hard work, intelligence, ingenuity, and a willingness to take risks. They are often portrayed as emblematic of the "American Dream," or the broader global belief that anyone, regardless of their background, can achieve extraordinary success if they work hard enough. The self-made billionaire myth reinforces the idea that our economic system is meritocratic, where rewards are distributed based on talent and effort.

However, a closer examination of how billionaires actually acquire their wealth reveals a much more complex and troubling reality. While billionaires may indeed possess intelligence, ambition, and a degree of hard work, their success is often built on a foundation of inherited wealth, monopolistic practices, tax avoidance, government subsidies, and, most importantly, the exploitation of labor. The myth of the self-made billionaire obscures the structural advantages that have contributed to their success and perpetuates a narrative that allows extreme wealth inequality to persist.

In this chapter, we will dissect the myth of the self-made billionaire by exploring real-life examples, examining the structural conditions that make such wealth accumulation possible, and challenging the idea that billionaires have "earned" their fortunes in a purely meritocratic sense.

The Role of Inherited Wealth

A significant number of billionaires owe their fortunes, at least in part, to inherited wealth. While these individuals may have expanded their family fortunes through business ventures or investments, the advantages they inherit give them a head start that most people could never hope to achieve. According to a 2019 report by Wealth-X, around 30% of billionaires globally inherited at least some of their wealth, while many others benefited from family connections and early access to capital, education, and networks that the average person lacks.

For example, consider the case of the Walton family, heirs to the Walmart fortune. Sam Walton, the founder of Walmart, built his company into one of the largest and most profitable retailers in the world. However, his children, who are among the wealthiest people on the planet, did not create or innovate anything to achieve their wealth. Instead, they inherited it. The wealth of the Walton family is now valued in the hundreds of billions, yet the narrative of their "success" overlooks the fact that their fortune was built on the labor of millions of Walmart employees, many of whom are paid low wages and receive minimal benefits.

Similarly, the Koch brothers, Charles and David Koch, inherited their wealth from their father, Fred Koch, who made his fortune in the oil industry. While the Koch brothers expanded the family business and became influential political players, their success was built on the foundation of inherited wealth. Their ability to use this wealth to influence politics, advocate for deregulation, and push policies that benefit their business interests further entrenched their economic power.

Even billionaires who are often considered "self-made" may have had significant help from inherited wealth or family connections. Take the case of Jeff Bezos, the founder of Amazon. While Bezos is often hailed as the quintessential self-made billionaire, his parents invested a significant amount of money in Amazon during its early days—reportedly around $300,000, a sum that would be out of reach for most aspiring entrepreneurs. While Bezos undoubtedly played a key role in Amazon's growth, his access to early capital gave him a substantial advantage over the average person attempting to start a business.

Corporate Monopolies and Market Domination

Another key factor in the accumulation of billionaire wealth is the ability to establish monopolistic or near-monopolistic control over key markets. In many cases, billionaires achieve their wealth not through fair competition or innovation, but by using their market power to stifle competitors, drive up prices, and exploit consumers and workers.

Amazon, again, serves as a prime example. While Jeff Bezos is often credited with revolutionizing e-commerce and creating a highly efficient logistics network, the company's success is also due in large part to its monopolistic practices. Amazon has been accused of using its dominant position in the market to crush competitors, both by undercutting prices and by leveraging its control over the platform to prioritize its own products over those of third-party sellers. Additionally, Amazon's relentless pursuit of market dominance has contributed to the erosion of wages and working conditions in the retail and logistics industries.

Similarly, tech giants like Google, Facebook, and Apple have used their dominant market positions to build enormous fortunes for their founders and executives. These companies control vast amounts of data, dominate online advertising markets, and have been accused of engaging in anti-competitive practices that stifle innovation and limit consumer choice. For example, Google has faced numerous antitrust investigations and lawsuits for allegedly using its control of search and advertising markets to crush competitors and maintain its dominance.

The wealth of billionaires in these industries is not the result of pure innovation or market competition. Instead, it is the product of monopolistic practices that allow these companies to extract value from consumers, workers, and smaller competitors. The concentration of wealth and power in the hands of a few billionaires is a direct consequence of their ability to dominate key markets and eliminate competition.

Tax Avoidance and Government Subsidies

Another factor that contributes to the accumulation of billionaire wealth is the ability to avoid paying taxes and take advantage of government subsidies. Billionaires, through their companies or personal finances, often use complex tax avoidance strategies to reduce their tax burden to levels far below what ordinary citizens pay. At the same time, many billionaires benefit from government subsidies, contracts, and bailouts that further enhance their wealth.

Tax avoidance is a common practice among the ultra-wealthy, who use a combination of offshore accounts, trusts, and other legal mechanisms to shield their wealth from taxation. For example, ProPublica's 2021 investigation into the taxes of American billionaires revealed that many of the wealthiest individuals in the country, including Jeff Bezos, Elon Musk, and Warren Buffett, paid little to no federal income taxes in certain years. While these individuals may not be breaking the law, their ability to exploit loopholes and take advantage of favorable tax policies allows them to accumulate wealth at a rate far greater than the average person.

Government subsidies also play a significant role in the fortunes of many billionaires. For example, Elon Musk, the founder of Tesla and SpaceX, has built much of his wealth on the back of government contracts and subsidies. Tesla, which produces electric vehicles, has benefited from billions of dollars in government incentives for clean energy development, while SpaceX has received lucrative contracts from NASA and the U.S. military. While Musk is often hailed as a visionary entrepreneur, his success is inextricably linked to government support, raising questions about the extent to which his wealth is truly "self-made."

In some cases, billionaires have also benefited from government bailouts that have protected their wealth during economic crises. For example, during the 2008 financial crisis, many billionaires in the banking and finance industries were bailed out by government interventions, such as the Troubled Asset Relief Program (TARP). While ordinary citizens lost their homes, jobs, and savings, many wealthy individuals and corporations were able to weather the storm with the help of government support, further entrenching their wealth and power.

The Exploitation of Labor

Perhaps the most significant factor in the accumulation of billionaire wealth is the exploitation of labor. While billionaires may be the public faces of their companies, the vast fortunes they accumulate are built on the backs of millions of workers who are often paid low wages, work in poor conditions, and have little job security. The myth of the self-made billionaire ignores the fact that wealth is not created in isolation—it is the product of collective labor, and billionaires disproportionately benefit from the labor of others.

Take, for example, the case of Amazon. While Jeff Bezos is often credited with building the company into a global retail giant, Amazon's success is built on the labor of hundreds of thousands of warehouse workers, delivery drivers, and other employees. These workers are often paid low wages, work in grueling conditions, and face constant pressure to meet demanding productivity targets. Amazon has faced numerous allegations of labor violations, including reports of workers being denied bathroom breaks, being injured on the job, and being subjected to intense surveillance and control.

Similarly, in industries like fast food, retail, and agriculture, billionaires accumulate wealth by paying their workers poverty-level wages while extracting enormous profits. For example, fast food magnates like the owners of McDonald's and Burger King have built their fortunes on the labor of low-wage workers, many of whom rely on government assistance to make ends meet. Meanwhile, these companies generate billions in revenue and reward their executives and shareholders with lavish compensation packages.

The exploitation of labor is not limited to low-wage industries. In sectors like technology, finance, and manufacturing, workers are often subjected to long hours, job insecurity, and high levels of stress, while the fruits of their labor are disproportionately funneled to the wealthiest individuals at the top. The ability of billionaires to extract value from the labor of others is a key driver of wealth inequality and challenges the notion that their success is solely the result of their own hard work or ingenuity.

Challenging the Meritocracy Myth

The myth of the self-made billionaire serves an important ideological function in justifying extreme wealth inequality. By portraying billionaires as individuals who have earned their fortunes through hard work, talent, and innovation, this narrative obscures the structural advantages that contribute to their success and downplays the role of exploitation, monopolistic practices, and government support.

Moreover, the self-made billionaire myth reinforces the idea that wealth inequality is a natural and inevitable outcome of a meritocratic system. If billionaires are simply the most talented and hardworking individuals in society, then their vast wealth is seen as a fair reward for their contributions. Conversely, those who struggle to make ends meet are often viewed as lacking the necessary qualities to succeed, perpetuating a culture of blame and individual responsibility.

However, as we have seen in this chapter, the reality is far more complex. Billionaire wealth is not the product of a fair and meritocratic system—it is the result of structural advantages, monopolistic practices, tax avoidance, government subsidies, and the exploitation of labor. Challenging the myth of the self-made billionaire is essential if we are to address the deep inequalities that plague our society and build a more just and equitable economic system.

Chapter 6: The Environmental Cost of Billionaires

The global environmental crisis, from climate change to biodiversity loss, has been one of the most pressing challenges of our time. It threatens the delicate balance of ecosystems, endangers human life, and destabilizes economies. At the center of this crisis is a glaring inequality: those who contribute the most to environmental degradation are often the wealthiest individuals and industries, while the most vulnerable populations bear the brunt of the consequences. Billionaires, by virtue of their concentrated wealth, have outsized ecological footprints, not only because of their personal consumption but also due to the industries they control and the policies they influence.

This chapter explores the environmental cost of billionaires, examining both the extravagant lifestyles they lead and the industries they dominate that contribute to environmental destruction. From private jets and mega-yachts to space tourism, the personal choices of billionaires have severe environmental consequences. But perhaps even more significant is the way that their investments and industries—such as fossil fuels, mining, and real estate—drive climate change, deforestation, and pollution on a global scale. Ultimately, this chapter makes the case that the existence of billionaires is not only an economic and ethical issue but an environmental one as well. Concentrated wealth in the hands of a few undermines global efforts to address climate change and protect ecosystems, creating a situation where the planet and its inhabitants suffer while the rich continue to prosper.

The Personal Ecological Footprint of Billionaires

While everyone has some impact on the environment, billionaires' personal lifestyles are marked by extravagance that far exceeds that of ordinary individuals. Their vast resources allow them to engage in consumption patterns that are inherently wasteful and damaging to the planet.

Private Jets and Mega-Yachts

One of the most visible symbols of billionaire wealth is the private jet. Owning or frequently flying in private jets allows billionaires to bypass commercial airlines and travel in luxury and convenience. However, private jets are among the most environmentally harmful modes of transportation. On average, a private jet emits up to 40 times more carbon dioxide per passenger than a commercial flight, which means that a single trip can produce more emissions than an entire household might in a year. According to a 2019 study by the European Federation for Transport and Environment, private jets emit as much as 10 times the carbon per passenger as regular air travel.

In addition to their high emissions, private jets also contribute to air pollution and noise pollution, affecting communities near airports and flight paths. Despite growing awareness of the climate crisis, the demand for private jets continues to rise, particularly among the ultra-wealthy. The COVID-19 pandemic, for instance, saw a surge in private jet use as billionaires sought to avoid commercial flights, further exacerbating their environmental impact.

Mega-yachts represent another significant source of environmental damage. These luxury vessels, often equipped with multiple decks, swimming pools, and even helicopter pads, consume vast amounts of fuel. A typical mega-yacht can emit around 7,000 tons of CO_2 per year, equivalent to the annual emissions of more than 1,000 average households. The construction and maintenance of these yachts also require significant resources, including rare materials and energy-intensive manufacturing processes.

Beyond their direct carbon emissions, mega-yachts contribute to marine pollution. These vessels release harmful chemicals into the water, including fuel, oil, and sewage, which can damage marine ecosystems and harm wildlife. Yachts often travel to pristine, ecologically sensitive areas, such as coral reefs and remote islands, where their presence disrupts local ecosystems and accelerates environmental degradation.

Space Tourism: The Ultimate Luxury and Environmental Cost

In recent years, a new frontier of billionaire extravagance has emerged: space tourism. Billionaires like Elon Musk, Jeff Bezos, and Richard Branson have invested billions of dollars in developing private spaceflight companies with the goal of commercializing space travel. While these ventures are often framed as innovative and futuristic, they also have a substantial environmental cost.

The rockets used for space tourism produce significant carbon emissions and other pollutants. While space flights are less frequent than air travel, the emissions per flight are far higher. For instance, a single suborbital space flight can emit more carbon than a typical car does in over a decade. Additionally, rockets release black carbon (soot) into the upper atmosphere, where it can linger for years and contribute to global warming by trapping heat.

Space tourism also raises ethical questions about the allocation of resources. At a time when the world is grappling with pressing environmental challenges, billions of dollars are being funneled into a luxury industry that benefits only the wealthiest individuals. The development of private spaceflight infrastructure, including spaceports and launch facilities, also has land use and environmental implications, particularly in rural or ecologically sensitive areas.

Industries Controlled by Billionaires: Driving Environmental Destruction

While the personal consumption patterns of billionaires are undoubtedly problematic, the industries they control have an even larger impact on the environment. Many billionaires derive their wealth from industries that are directly responsible for environmental degradation, including fossil fuels, mining, and real estate development. These industries contribute to climate change, deforestation, pollution, and the depletion of natural resources on a massive scale.

Fossil Fuels: A Billionaire's Goldmine

The fossil fuel industry has long been a source of immense wealth for billionaires, particularly in the oil, gas, and coal sectors. However, it is also one of the leading contributors to climate change and environmental destruction. Burning fossil fuels releases greenhouse gases, primarily carbon dioxide, into the atmosphere, driving global warming and altering weather patterns. The extraction of fossil fuels—whether through drilling, fracking, or mining—also causes significant environmental harm, including habitat destruction, water pollution, and air pollution.

Many of the world's richest individuals have built their fortunes in the fossil fuel industry, including members of the Saudi royal family, the Koch brothers in the United States, and Russian oligarchs like Roman Abramovich. These billionaires have a vested interest in maintaining the status quo and often use their wealth and political influence to resist efforts to transition to renewable energy. For example, the Koch brothers have spent hundreds of millions of dollars funding climate denial campaigns, lobbying against environmental regulations, and supporting politicians who oppose action on climate change.

The continued dominance of fossil fuel billionaires poses a significant barrier to addressing the climate crisis. As long as these individuals and their companies remain powerful and profitable, they will have little incentive to support policies that would reduce emissions or shift toward cleaner energy sources. The result is a system where short-term profits for a few billionaires come at the expense of long-term environmental sustainability for the planet.

Mining: Extracting Wealth, Depleting the Earth

The mining industry is another source of wealth for many billionaires, but it is also one of the most environmentally destructive industries in the world. Mining for minerals, metals, and fossil fuels often involves large-scale deforestation, habitat destruction, and the contamination of soil and water sources. The extraction of rare metals used in electronics, for example, can have devastating ecological consequences, including the displacement of communities, loss of biodiversity, and the creation of toxic waste.

Billionaires like Gina Rinehart, one of Australia's wealthiest individuals, have made their fortunes in the mining industry. Rinehart's company, Hancock Prospecting, operates some of the largest iron ore mines in the world. However, her business has also been linked to environmental controversies, including the destruction of Aboriginal lands and the degradation of sensitive ecosystems.

Mining billionaires often operate in countries with weak environmental regulations, allowing them to exploit natural resources with little regard for the long-term environmental consequences. The financial incentives for mining are immense, and as long as demand for minerals and metals remains high, billionaires in the industry will continue to extract wealth from the earth, leaving environmental devastation in their wake.

Real Estate Development: Building Over Nature

The real estate industry, controlled by many billionaires, also plays a significant role in environmental degradation. Real estate development often involves the destruction of natural habitats to make way for housing, commercial properties, and infrastructure. Urban sprawl, in particular, contributes to deforestation, the loss of agricultural land, and increased carbon emissions from transportation.

Billionaires like Donald Trump and Hong Kong's Li Ka-shing have amassed enormous wealth through real estate ventures, but their projects often prioritize profit over environmental sustainability. Large-scale developments can strain local resources, increase energy consumption, and contribute to air and water pollution. In many cases, real estate billionaires lobby against environmental regulations that would limit their ability to build on ecologically sensitive lands.

The environmental impact of real estate development is not limited to the construction phase. Many developments are designed with little consideration for energy efficiency or sustainable practices, leading to higher long-term environmental costs. For example, luxury resorts, high-end shopping malls, and sprawling residential communities often require vast amounts of water and energy to maintain, contributing to the depletion of natural resources and increased carbon emissions.

Philanthropy and "Greenwashing": The Billionaire's Response to Environmental Criticism

THE BILLIONAIRE LIMIT

In recent years, many billionaires have sought to improve their public image by engaging in environmental philanthropy or investing in "green" industries. While these efforts are often framed as a way for billionaires to give back to society, they are frequently criticized as forms of "greenwashing"—superficial attempts to appear environmentally responsible without addressing the root causes of environmental destruction.

For example, Bill Gates has positioned himself as a leader in the fight against climate change through his investments in renewable energy and his advocacy for technological solutions to reduce emissions. However, critics argue that Gates' approach focuses too much on technological fixes while ignoring the need for systemic changes to the economic system that allows billionaires to accumulate wealth at the expense of the environment. Moreover, some of the industries that have made Gates a billionaire, such as technology and agriculture, are themselves contributors to environmental degradation.

Similarly, Jeff Bezos has pledged billions of dollars to combat climate change through the Bezos Earth Fund. However, this philanthropic effort is dwarfed by the environmental impact of Amazon, the company that made him one of the richest individuals in the world. Amazon's global shipping network, data centers, and reliance on fossil fuels contribute significantly to carbon emissions and environmental degradation. Bezos' personal consumption habits, including his use of private jets and plans for space tourism, further undermine his claims of environmental responsibility.

While billionaire philanthropy can provide funding for important environmental initiatives, it is often insufficient to address the scale of the environmental crisis. Furthermore, these efforts do little to challenge the underlying economic system that enables billionaires to profit from environmental destruction in the first place. In many cases, philanthropy serves as a way for billionaires to deflect criticism and maintain their wealth and influence while continuing to engage in environmentally harmful practices.

The Case for Redistributing Wealth to Save the Planet

The environmental cost of billionaires is clear: their extravagant lifestyles, industries, and political influence all contribute to the degradation of the planet. Addressing the environmental crisis requires not only technological solutions and policy reforms but also a fundamental shift in how wealth is distributed and how the economy is structured.

Redistributing wealth from billionaires to the broader population could have significant environmental benefits. By reducing the concentration of wealth, we could decrease the demand for environmentally harmful luxury goods and services, such as private jets and space tourism. Furthermore, redistributing wealth would allow for greater investment in public goods, such as renewable energy, public transportation, and conservation efforts.

In addition to reducing consumption, a more equitable distribution of wealth could help address the environmental injustices that disproportionately affect low-income communities. Many of the people most vulnerable to the effects of climate change, pollution, and resource depletion are those who have the least access to wealth and resources. By redistributing wealth, we could provide these communities with the resources they need to adapt to a changing climate and protect their environments.

Ultimately, the environmental crisis cannot be solved without addressing the economic inequality that allows billionaires to profit from environmental destruction. Concentrated wealth in the hands of a few individuals creates a system where short-term profits are prioritized over long-term sustainability, and where the needs of the planet are secondary to the desires of the rich. By challenging the existence of billionaires and redistributing wealth, we can create a more sustainable and just world for future generations.

Chapter 7: How Billionaires Exploit Workers

The concentration of wealth in the hands of billionaires is not merely the product of savvy investments, visionary ideas, or technological innovation. Rather, it is the result of a system that systematically undervalues labor and prioritizes profit over people. At the heart of the billionaire phenomenon is a fundamental imbalance: while workers create the value that drives companies forward, they often see little benefit from the profits that are generated. Instead, the vast majority of these profits are funneled upwards to a small group of individuals—billionaires—who benefit from practices that exploit labor on a massive scale.

This chapter digs into how billionaires accumulate their wealth by underpaying workers, minimizing benefits, and resisting labor rights movements. By examining major industries such as retail, manufacturing, technology, and the gig economy, we will explore how employees often endure poor working conditions, stagnant wages, and precarious employment, even as the wealth of billionaires grows. We will also discuss how globalization, outsourcing, and automation have furthered this divide, concentrating wealth in the hands of a few while leaving workers behind.

The Foundations of Worker Exploitation

Exploitation of workers is a common feature across many industries that have created billionaires. It manifests in various forms, including low wages, poor working conditions, lack of benefits, and the suppression of unions. By keeping labor costs as low as possible, billionaires and their corporations maximize profits, often at the expense of the workers who are essential to the success of their businesses.

Wage Suppression and Inequality

One of the most obvious ways in which billionaires exploit workers is through wage suppression. While the productivity of workers has increased significantly over the past few decades, wages for the vast majority of employees have stagnated or even declined in real terms. According to data from the Economic Policy Institute, between 1979 and 2020, worker productivity grew by more than 60%, but the average hourly pay for non-supervisory workers increased by only about 17%. In contrast, the compensation of CEOs and other executives—many of whom are billionaires or on their way to becoming so—has skyrocketed.

This growing wage gap has been fueled by several factors. First, the decline of labor unions in many countries, particularly the United States, has weakened workers' ability to bargain for better pay and working conditions. Billionaires and their corporations have played an active role in this decline, opposing unionization efforts and lobbying for policies that restrict workers' rights to organize. For example, companies like Amazon, Walmart, and McDonald's have been notorious for their anti-union activities, often engaging in aggressive tactics to prevent workers from organizing.

At the same time, globalization and outsourcing have allowed corporations to shift production to countries where labor is cheaper and workers have fewer rights. This has enabled companies to further suppress wages in their home countries by threatening to move jobs overseas if workers demand higher pay or better benefits. The result is a global race to the bottom, where workers in both developed and developing countries are pitted against each other in a bid to offer the lowest wages and the most flexible, precarious employment conditions.

Poor Working Conditions

Along with wage suppression, billionaires and their corporations often subject workers to poor and unsafe working conditions. This is particularly evident in industries such as retail, manufacturing, and agriculture, where workers are often required to work long hours for low pay in environments that pose significant risks to their health and safety.

For example, the garment industry—an industry that has produced billionaires such as Amancio Ortega, the founder of Zara—has long been notorious for its reliance on sweatshops. In countries like Bangladesh, Vietnam, and Cambodia, garment workers are often paid poverty wages to work in overcrowded, poorly ventilated factories. Many of these factories lack basic safety measures, leading to tragedies such as the 2013 Rana Plaza collapse in Bangladesh, which killed more than 1,100 workers and injured thousands more.

Closer to home, workers in the retail sector face their own challenges. Billionaire-owned companies such as Walmart and

Amazon have been widely criticized for subjecting employees to grueling work schedules, unrealistic productivity targets, and punitive management practices. Amazon warehouse workers, for example, have reported being constantly monitored by management, with bathroom breaks and downtime tightly controlled. Many workers are pushed to the brink of exhaustion, leading to high rates of injury and turnover.

In the agricultural sector, workers—many of whom are migrants or undocumented—are often exposed to hazardous chemicals, extreme weather conditions, and exploitative labor practices. Billionaires in the agribusiness industry, such as the owners of large-scale farms and food processing companies, benefit from this cheap and vulnerable labor force while resisting efforts to improve working conditions or provide basic protections for workers.

Lack of Benefits and Job Security

In addition to low wages and poor working conditions, many workers employed by billionaire-owned corporations face a lack of benefits and job security. Part-time and temporary employment has become increasingly common in industries such as retail, hospitality, and manufacturing, allowing companies to avoid providing benefits such as health insurance, paid leave, and retirement savings.

Billionaires and their companies have been instrumental in pushing for this shift towards precarious employment. For instance, the rise of "just-in-time" scheduling in retail, where workers' hours are determined based on fluctuating demand, has allowed companies to cut labor costs by reducing the number of full-time employees. This practice, which is common at companies like Walmart and McDonald's, leaves workers with unpredictable schedules and little financial stability.

The rise of the gig economy, which we will explore in greater detail later in this chapter, has further exacerbated this trend. Platforms like Uber, Lyft, and DoorDash—whose founders and investors have become billionaires—rely on a workforce of independent contractors who are not entitled to the benefits and protections that come with traditional employment. This model allows companies to avoid paying for health insurance, retirement benefits, or workers' compensation, shifting the financial burden onto workers who are already struggling to make ends meet.

Globalization, Outsourcing, and the Race to the Bottom

Globalization and outsourcing have played a key role in the exploitation of workers by billionaires and their corporations. By shifting production to countries with lower labor costs and fewer labor protections, billionaires have been able to maximize profits while driving down wages and working conditions for workers in both developed and developing countries.

The Global Supply Chain and the Exploitation of Workers

The global supply chain has become a central feature of the modern economy, with goods produced in one part of the world and sold in another. Billionaires who own multinational corporations have used this system to their advantage, moving production to countries where labor is cheap, environmental regulations are lax, and workers have little power to demand better wages or working conditions.

For example, companies like Nike, Apple, and H&M have been able to increase their profit margins by outsourcing production to countries like China, Vietnam, and Bangladesh, where workers are paid a fraction of what they would earn in developed countries. These companies often rely on subcontractors, allowing them to distance themselves from the poor labor conditions in their supply chains. However, the reality is that billionaires at the top of these companies are profiting from a system that exploits workers in the developing world, many of whom are trapped in low-wage jobs with little opportunity for advancement.

The exploitation of workers in the global supply chain is not limited to the developing world. In the United States and other developed countries, the threat of outsourcing has been used as a tool to suppress wages and weaken labor unions. Companies that threaten to move production overseas if workers demand higher wages or better benefits create a climate of fear and insecurity, making it difficult for workers to organize and advocate for their rights.

The Role of Trade Agreements and Corporate Influence

Trade agreements have played a significant role in facilitating globalization and outsourcing, allowing billionaires and their corporations to move production across borders with ease. Many of these agreements have been designed with the interests of multinational corporations in mind, prioritizing the free flow of capital and goods over the rights of workers and the protection of the environment.

For example, the North American Free Trade Agreement (NAFTA), which came into effect in 1994, was hailed as a victory for free trade and economic growth. However, it also had devastating consequences for workers in both the United States and Mexico. In the U.S., NAFTA led to the outsourcing of manufacturing jobs to Mexico, where labor costs were lower and environmental regulations were weaker. This hollowed out many American manufacturing towns, leading to job losses and economic decline. Meanwhile, in Mexico, workers in the maquiladora factories that sprung up along the border were paid low wages and subjected to poor working conditions, with little recourse to improve their situation.

Billionaires and their corporations have been key players in shaping these trade agreements, using their political influence to push for policies that benefit their bottom line. Through lobbying and campaign contributions, they have ensured that the global economic system is designed to prioritize corporate profits over the well-being of workers.

Automation and the Future of Work

As if the challenges posed by globalization and outsourcing were not enough, workers today are also facing the threat of automation. Billionaires in the technology and manufacturing sectors have invested heavily in automation, driven by the desire to reduce labor costs and increase efficiency. While automation has the potential to improve productivity and reduce the need for dangerous or repetitive jobs, it also raises significant concerns about job displacement and the future of work.

The Impact of Automation on Low-Wage Workers

The rise of automation has already begun to displace workers in industries such as manufacturing, retail, and transportation. Robots, artificial intelligence, and machine learning have enabled companies to automate tasks that were once performed by human workers, leading to job losses and reduced demand for low-wage labor.

For example, in the manufacturing sector, billionaires like Elon Musk have invested in highly automated factories that require fewer human workers. While these innovations may improve efficiency and reduce production costs, they also contribute to job losses in traditional manufacturing industries, leaving workers with fewer opportunities for stable, well-paying jobs.

In the retail sector, companies like Amazon have introduced automation in their warehouses, using robots to pick and pack items for shipment. This has allowed the company to reduce its reliance on human labor, even as it continues to expand its operations. While Amazon's use of automation has enabled it to become one of the most valuable companies in the world, it has also contributed to job losses and wage stagnation for warehouse workers.

The Gig Economy and the Rise of Precarious Work

At the same time that automation is displacing workers, the rise of the gig economy is creating a new class of precarious, low-wage jobs. Platforms like Uber, Lyft, and DoorDash have revolutionized the way people work, offering flexible, on-demand jobs that allow workers to earn money on their own schedule. However, these jobs come with significant drawbacks, including low pay, lack of benefits, and little job security.

The gig economy has been hailed as a disruptive force that empowers workers to be their own bosses. However, the reality is that the gig economy often benefits billionaires at the expense of workers. The founders and investors behind these platforms have become billionaires by extracting value from a workforce of independent contractors who are not entitled to the same protections as traditional employees. Gig workers are responsible for their own expenses, such as gas, insurance, and maintenance, and they do not receive benefits like health insurance or retirement savings.

Furthermore, the gig economy relies on algorithms and data to manage its workforce, allowing companies to control workers' schedules and pay rates without direct oversight. This creates a power imbalance, where gig workers have little control over their working conditions and are vulnerable to sudden changes in pay or job availability.

The Need for Structural Change

THE BILLIONAIRE LIMIT

The exploitation of workers is a central feature of the billionaire economy. Through wage suppression, poor working conditions, precarious employment, and the threat of automation and outsourcing, billionaires have been able to amass vast fortunes while leaving workers behind. This exploitation is not an unfortunate byproduct of capitalism—it is a deliberate strategy that allows billionaires and their corporations to maximize profits at the expense of the people who create the wealth.

Addressing this exploitation requires more than just individual reforms or adjustments to the system—it requires a fundamental restructuring of the economy to prioritize workers' rights and ensure that the wealth generated by labor is shared more equitably. This means strengthening labor unions, raising the minimum wage, providing universal benefits such as healthcare and paid leave, and ensuring that workers have a voice in the decisions that affect their lives. It also means challenging the concentration of wealth and power in the hands of a few individuals and creating a system where the needs of workers are prioritized over the desires of billionaires.

By addressing the exploitation of workers, we can begin to build an economy that works for everyone, not just the wealthy few.

Chapter 8: Wealth Limits: Historical and International Perspectives

Throughout history, societies have grappled with the challenge of wealth concentration, recognizing that unchecked accumulation of resources by a small elite poses significant threats to both social cohesion and economic stability. Limiting wealth through progressive taxation, anti-monopoly laws, and various regulatory mechanisms has been a recurring theme in public policy debates. This chapter explores the history of wealth limits and progressive taxation, examining successful examples from different countries and eras. By delving into policies such as wealth taxes, inheritance taxes, and anti-monopoly regulations, we aim to show how these measures have been used to curb inequality and promote social welfare. Additionally, the chapter looks at modern societies with varying approaches to wealth concentration, offering a comparative analysis of international models and the lessons that can be learned.

Historical Roots of Wealth Limits

The idea of limiting excessive wealth is not a new phenomenon. Long before modern taxation systems, ancient societies recognized the need to curb the accumulation of wealth to prevent social instability. In these societies, wealth limits were often tied to moral, religious, or cultural beliefs about fairness, justice, and the collective good.

THE BILLIONAIRE LIMIT

Ancient Civilizations and Wealth Redistribution

In ancient Greece, philosopher Aristotle argued that excessive wealth concentration was harmful to the state, as it bred inequality and social discord. Aristotle believed that a balance between extreme wealth and poverty was necessary for the health of a functioning democracy. His views were echoed by the Roman Republic, which saw land reforms aimed at redistributing wealth. One notable example was the Lex Licinia Sextia, a Roman law passed in 367 BCE that aimed to limit the amount of public land one person could own. The law was introduced in response to the concentration of land among wealthy elites, which was contributing to growing inequality and unrest.

The idea of wealth limits also found expression in early religious traditions. For example, in the Jewish tradition, the practice of "jubilee" mandated the redistribution of land every 50 years to prevent long-term inequality and ensure that families could maintain a livelihood. Similarly, early Islamic society introduced the practice of *zakat*, a form of almsgiving that functioned as a wealth tax to provide for the poor and needy. These ancient examples highlight the widespread recognition that unchecked wealth accumulation poses risks to social stability and equity.

Medieval and Early Modern Europe: Wealth and Power

During the Middle Ages in Europe, the concentration of wealth was closely tied to land ownership, with a feudal system that saw landowners amassing vast estates while peasants lived in poverty. In response to this inequality, medieval rulers occasionally imposed wealth limits through land redistribution, taxation, or other policies designed to maintain social harmony. For instance, in medieval England, the Statute of Mortmain (1279) was enacted to prevent the transfer of land to the church, which was accumulating large tracts of property, making it harder for the Crown to tax or control wealth. This early example of an anti-monopoly law highlights the recognition that unchecked wealth accumulation by a single entity could undermine state power.

Moving into the early modern period, with the rise of mercantilism and the expansion of global trade, European monarchies became increasingly concerned about the concentration of wealth in the hands of private individuals and corporations. This concern was particularly acute with the rise of trading companies like the British East India Company and the Dutch East India Company, which held monopolistic power over vast regions and resources. In response, European states introduced a range of policies to regulate wealth concentration, including tariffs, trade restrictions, and, eventually, progressive taxation systems.

The Birth of Progressive Taxation

The concept of progressive taxation—whereby the wealthy are taxed at higher rates than the poor—emerged in the 19th century as a response to the rapid industrialization and growing inequality of the time. The Industrial Revolution had created vast fortunes for factory owners, while working-class citizens faced poverty, long hours, and dangerous conditions.

THE BILLIONAIRE LIMIT

As inequality widened, social unrest and demands for reform grew, prompting governments to consider ways to reduce the gap between rich and poor.

The Early 20th Century: Wealth Limits and Social Reform

The early 20th century saw significant efforts to limit wealth concentration, particularly in response to the economic crises of the time. In the aftermath of World War I, many countries introduced progressive income taxes, capital gains taxes, and inheritance taxes as a way to prevent the excessive accumulation of wealth and promote social welfare.

One of the most notable examples of wealth limits during this period was the introduction of the estate tax in the United States. First enacted in 1916, the estate tax was designed to prevent the creation of a permanent aristocracy by taxing the transfer of wealth from one generation to the next. In his support for the tax, President Theodore Roosevelt argued that "the absence of effective State, and, especially, national, restraint upon unfair money-getting has tended to create a small class of enormously wealthy and economically powerful men, whose chief object is to hold and increase their power."

Following the Great Depression, wealth limits became an even more central part of public policy, particularly in the United States and Europe. In response to the widespread poverty and economic collapse of the 1930s, governments introduced a range of social reforms aimed at redistributing wealth and preventing future crises. The New Deal in the United States, for example, included significant tax increases on the wealthy, as well as regulations designed to prevent the concentration of economic power in the hands of a few corporations.

During this period, the top marginal tax rate in the United States reached as high as 94% under President Franklin D. Roosevelt, a level of taxation designed not only to raise revenue but also to limit the accumulation of wealth by the richest Americans. Similar policies were enacted across Europe, where social democratic governments introduced wealth taxes, inheritance taxes, and anti-monopoly laws to curb inequality and promote social welfare.

International Models of Wealth Limits

While the United States and Europe were pioneers in progressive taxation and wealth redistribution in the 20th century, other countries have also experimented with wealth limits and anti-monopoly measures. These international models offer valuable lessons for how wealth concentration can be managed in different cultural and economic contexts.

The Nordic Model: Social Welfare and High Taxes

The Nordic countries—Denmark, Sweden, Norway, Finland, and Iceland—are often cited as examples of societies that have successfully limited wealth concentration while maintaining high levels of social welfare. These countries have implemented progressive tax systems that include high income taxes, wealth taxes, and inheritance taxes. In return, they offer extensive social benefits such as free education, universal healthcare, and generous unemployment benefits.

The success of the Nordic model is often attributed to the strong social contract that exists between citizens and the state. In these countries, there is a widespread belief that wealth should be shared more equitably and that the state has a responsibility to provide for the common good. This cultural norm has made it politically feasible to maintain high tax rates on the wealthy, even as globalization and technological change have created new opportunities for wealth accumulation.

In Sweden, for example, the top marginal tax rate on income is 57%, while wealth taxes and inheritance taxes further limit the accumulation of wealth by the richest citizens. Despite these high tax rates, Sweden has a thriving economy with high levels of innovation, entrepreneurship, and economic growth. This demonstrates that limiting wealth through progressive taxation does not necessarily stifle economic dynamism or individual initiative. Rather, it can create a more stable and equitable society where everyone has the opportunity to succeed.

Germany: Anti-Monopoly Regulations and Wealth Redistribution

Germany offers another example of a country that has successfully limited wealth concentration through a combination of progressive taxation and strict anti-monopoly regulations. After World War II, Germany underwent a period of significant economic reform, including the introduction of policies designed to prevent the concentration of wealth and power in the hands of a few large corporations.

One of the key features of the German economic model is the system of "co-determination," which requires large companies to include worker representatives on their boards of directors. This system helps to ensure that workers have a say in corporate decision-making and prevents the excessive concentration of power in the hands of wealthy shareholders and executives.

Germany has also maintained a progressive tax system that includes high income taxes, capital gains taxes, and inheritance taxes. In recent years, there has been growing debate about the need for a wealth tax to further limit the concentration of wealth in the hands of the country's richest citizens. While the wealth tax was abolished in 1997, many Germans support its reintroduction as a way to address rising inequality and ensure that the country's economic success is shared more broadly.

Japan: Post-War Reforms and Land Redistribution

In the aftermath of World War II, Japan underwent a series of radical economic reforms designed to prevent the concentration of wealth and promote social welfare. One of the most significant of these reforms was the redistribution of land, which broke up large estates and provided small farmers with the opportunity to own their own land. This policy helped to reduce rural poverty and prevent the emergence of a landed aristocracy, which had been a significant source of inequality in pre-war Japan.

In addition to land reform, Japan introduced progressive income taxes and inheritance taxes designed to limit the accumulation of wealth by the country's richest citizens. These policies helped to create a more equitable distribution of wealth and contributed to Japan's rapid economic recovery in the post-war period.

While Japan has experienced rising inequality in recent decades, the country continues to maintain a relatively progressive tax system and strong social safety nets. The lessons of Japan's post-war reforms offer valuable insights into how wealth limits can be used to promote social stability and economic growth in the aftermath of a major crisis.

Lessons Learned from Historical and International Models

The historical and international examples discussed in this chapter offer valuable lessons for how wealth limits can be used to curb inequality and promote social welfare. These lessons are particularly relevant in the context of rising inequality and the concentration of wealth in the hands of billionaires in the 21st century.

First, these examples show that wealth limits are not a new or radical idea. Societies throughout history have recognized the dangers of excessive wealth concentration and have implemented policies to prevent it. Whether through progressive taxation, land reform, or anti-monopoly regulations, these policies have been used to promote social stability and ensure that wealth is shared more equitably.

Second, these examples demonstrate that wealth limits do not necessarily stifle economic growth or innovation. On the contrary, countries like Sweden, Germany, and Japan have shown that it is possible to limit wealth concentration while maintaining a dynamic and prosperous economy. By ensuring that wealth is distributed more fairly, these countries have created more stable and equitable societies where everyone has the opportunity to succeed.

Finally, the historical and international models discussed in this chapter highlight the importance of political will and cultural norms in implementing wealth limits. In many cases, the success of these policies has depended on strong public support for the idea that wealth should be shared more equitably and that the state has a responsibility to provide for the common good. This cultural norm has made it possible to maintain high tax rates on the wealthy and implement other policies designed to curb inequality.

The Path Forward

As we face the challenges of the 21st century, it is clear that the concentration of wealth in the hands of a few billionaires poses significant risks to both social stability and economic growth. The historical and international examples discussed in this chapter offer valuable insights into how wealth limits can be used to address these challenges and promote a more equitable distribution of wealth.

By implementing policies such as progressive taxation, wealth taxes, and anti-monopoly regulations, we can begin to limit the excessive accumulation of wealth and ensure that the benefits of economic growth are shared more broadly. These policies are not only necessary for promoting social justice but also for creating a more stable and prosperous society where everyone has the opportunity to succeed.

Chapter 9: Why Philanthropy Isn't the Answer

In the modern era, philanthropy has been widely promoted as a solution to the world's most pressing social, economic, and environmental problems. Some of the wealthiest individuals in the world, including high-profile billionaires like Bill Gates, Warren Buffet, and Elon Musk, have championed charitable giving as a means of addressing issues such as poverty, healthcare, and education. Their contributions are often celebrated as acts of goodwill, generosity, and moral responsibility. However, beneath the surface of this seemingly altruistic practice lies a more complex and problematic reality.

This chapter argues that billionaire philanthropy, while sometimes well-intentioned, is not the answer to the structural issues of inequality and injustice in society. While philanthropic efforts may alleviate some symptoms of social problems, they do little to address their root causes. More importantly, billionaire philanthropy often comes with strings attached, promotes personal agendas, and serves as a way to avoid taxes while maintaining power. It can also undermine public institutions, shifting the responsibility for addressing social issues from governments and democratically accountable institutions to a small group of ultra-wealthy individuals. In this chapter, we will explore the fundamental flaws in relying on philanthropy as a solution to the inequities caused by wealth concentration and discuss why more systemic changes are necessary to create a just and equitable society.

THE BILLIONAIRE LIMIT

The Myth of the Benevolent Billionaire

One of the most pervasive myths surrounding billionaire philanthropy is the idea that wealthy individuals are uniquely qualified to solve society's problems because of their intelligence, success, and entrepreneurial spirit. This myth portrays billionaires as benevolent figures who have earned their wealth through hard work and innovation and who now wish to give back to society. However, this narrative overlooks the fact that the accumulation of extreme wealth often depends on systems of exploitation, inequality, and privilege. It also ignores the ways in which philanthropy can serve as a tool for the rich to maintain and enhance their influence and power.

The idea of the "benevolent billionaire" is rooted in the notion that private charity is a more efficient and effective way to address social problems than government intervention. Proponents of this view argue that billionaires, through their businesses, have already demonstrated their ability to innovate and solve problems, and thus they are better equipped to tackle complex social issues than bureaucratic and inefficient governments. This argument assumes that billionaires are motivated by altruism and the desire to improve the world rather than by personal gain or the desire to exert influence over public life.

However, the reality is more complicated. While some billionaires may genuinely seek to address social problems through their philanthropic efforts, the practice of billionaire philanthropy is often closely tied to self-interest. Many billionaires use philanthropy as a way to enhance their public image, protect their wealth from taxation, and promote their personal or ideological agendas. In doing so, they can shape public policy and social outcomes in ways that serve their own interests, rather than the needs of society as a whole.

Philanthropy and Power: Shaping Agendas

One of the central problems with billionaire philanthropy is the concentration of power it represents. When a handful of wealthy individuals control vast amounts of financial resources, they also gain disproportionate influence over the causes and issues that receive attention and funding. This allows billionaires to shape the public agenda in ways that reflect their own priorities and values, rather than those of the broader population.

For example, when billionaires like Bill Gates or Mark Zuckerberg make large donations to education reform or global health initiatives, they are not simply contributing to a public good—they are actively shaping the direction of those fields. Their philanthropic foundations wield significant power over how resources are allocated, which projects are funded, and which solutions are pursued. In some cases, this can lead to positive outcomes, but it also raises serious concerns about accountability and democracy.

When billionaires use their wealth to influence social outcomes, they often do so without the input or oversight of the communities they are ostensibly helping. This can result in philanthropic efforts that are disconnected from the real needs and desires of those communities. For instance, in the field of education, billionaire philanthropists have often promoted controversial reforms such as charter schools or standardized testing, which have been criticized for undermining public education and exacerbating inequalities. In these cases, the decisions about how to "improve" education are made by wealthy individuals and their foundations, rather than by educators, parents, or students themselves.

Moreover, the agendas promoted by billionaire philanthropists are often aligned with their own financial interests. Many billionaires focus their philanthropy on causes that reinforce the systems and industries from which they have benefited. For example, tech billionaires may prioritize funding for digital education initiatives or artificial intelligence research, fields that are closely tied to their own businesses and investments. In doing so, they are able to promote their own industries and potentially profit from the solutions they fund, all under the guise of charitable giving.

The Tax Avoidance Strategy

Philanthropy is not only a way for billionaires to shape the public agenda—it is also a tool for avoiding taxes. In many countries, charitable donations are tax-deductible, meaning that billionaires can reduce their tax liability by giving away a portion of their wealth to philanthropic causes. While this may seem like a fair trade-off—after all, the money is being used for charitable purposes—it raises serious concerns about fairness and the role of government in redistributing wealth.

When billionaires use philanthropy to reduce their taxes, they are effectively privatizing the decision-making process about how public resources should be allocated. Instead of paying taxes, which would go to democratically accountable governments to fund public services such as healthcare, education, and infrastructure, billionaires are able to direct their money to the causes of their choosing. This undermines the idea of taxation as a collective responsibility and weakens the ability of governments to address social problems in a systematic and equitable way.

Furthermore, the tax deductions associated with philanthropy disproportionately benefit the wealthy. The more money a billionaire gives away, the more they can reduce their tax burden, effectively lowering their tax rate compared to ordinary citizens. This creates a situation where the richest individuals in society are able to avoid paying their fair share of taxes, while ordinary workers continue to bear the burden of funding public services. It also means that public resources are diverted from democratically accountable institutions, such as governments, to private foundations and charities controlled by billionaires.

The tax benefits of philanthropy are further compounded by the fact that many billionaires set up charitable foundations, which allow them to maintain control over their wealth while still reaping the tax benefits of charitable giving. Foundations are often structured in ways that allow their founders to retain significant influence over how their money is spent, even after it has been donated. In some cases, billionaires even use foundations to fund projects that directly benefit their own businesses or interests. For example, a billionaire might donate to a foundation that funds research or development in an industry where they have significant investments, creating a circular flow of wealth that ultimately benefits the donor.

Philanthropy as a Substitute for Public Responsibility

One of the most concerning aspects of billionaire philanthropy is the way it can undermine public institutions and government responsibility. By relying on the charitable donations of billionaires to address social problems, society shifts the burden of solving these problems from the government to private individuals. This can lead to a weakening of public services and a reduction in the accountability of government institutions.

For example, when billionaires donate to public education, they are often stepping in to fill gaps left by underfunded government programs. While this may seem like a positive contribution, it can also create a dependency on private philanthropy to fund essential services. Over time, this can lead to a situation where public institutions are reliant on the goodwill of wealthy individuals to function, rather than being adequately funded through public taxation. This weakens the social contract between citizens and the state and erodes the notion that governments are responsible for providing basic services and addressing social inequality.

Moreover, billionaire philanthropy can distort the priorities of public institutions. When private donors contribute large sums of money to public universities, hospitals, or museums, they often attach conditions to their donations. This can lead to public institutions prioritizing the interests of their wealthy donors over the needs of the broader population. For example, a university that receives a large donation from a billionaire may be pressured to invest in specific research areas or build facilities that align with the donor's interests, even if those projects do not serve the needs of students or faculty.

This dynamic is particularly troubling in sectors like healthcare, where billionaire philanthropy can have a direct impact on public health outcomes. For instance, when billionaires donate to global health initiatives, they often fund specific diseases or treatments that align with their personal interests, rather than addressing broader systemic issues like healthcare infrastructure or access to basic services. This can result in a misallocation of resources, where certain diseases or populations receive disproportionate attention and funding, while other pressing health issues are neglected.

The Limits of Charity: Addressing Symptoms, Not Causes

At its core, the problem with relying on philanthropy to solve social problems is that it tends to address the symptoms of inequality, rather than its root causes. Philanthropic efforts are often focused on providing immediate relief to those in need, whether through food banks, scholarships, or healthcare initiatives. While these efforts can provide important support to individuals and communities in crisis, they do little to address the underlying structural issues that perpetuate inequality and injustice.

For example, a billionaire might donate money to fund scholarships for low-income students, helping a select group of individuals access higher education. While this is undoubtedly beneficial for the students who receive the scholarships, it does not address the broader issues of education inequality, such as underfunded public schools, rising tuition costs, or systemic barriers to college access for marginalized groups. Similarly, a billionaire might fund a program to provide healthcare in underserved communities, but this does not address the deeper issues of healthcare access, affordability, and quality that affect millions of people.

In many cases, philanthropy can actually perpetuate the very systems of inequality that it seeks to address. By providing targeted assistance to a select group of individuals, philanthropic efforts can create a "band-aid" solution that alleviates immediate suffering but leaves the broader structures of inequality intact. Moreover, by focusing on charitable giving as the primary solution to social problems, society can become complacent in addressing the systemic issues that create inequality in the first place.

The Need for Systemic Change

While philanthropy can provide important support to individuals and communities in need, it is not a substitute for systemic change. The concentration of wealth in the hands of a few billionaires is a symptom of a larger problem—the structural inequalities that exist in our economic, political, and social systems. Addressing these issues requires more than charitable donations; it requires a fundamental rethinking of how wealth is distributed, how public resources are allocated, and how social problems are addressed.

Rather than relying on the goodwill of billionaires to solve society's problems, we must focus on creating a system in which wealth is more equitably distributed, and public institutions are adequately funded to address the needs of all citizens. This means implementing policies such as progressive taxation, wealth taxes, and stronger regulations on corporate power and monopolies. It also means investing in public services like education, healthcare, and infrastructure, so that all individuals have access to the resources they need to thrive.

Ultimately, the answer to inequality and injustice is not philanthropy—it is a fair and just system that ensures that everyone has the opportunity to succeed, regardless of their wealth or status.

Chapter 10: How to Set a Billionaire Limit

As the gap between the wealthy elite and the rest of society grows ever wider, the question of how much wealth is too much becomes more pressing. The unchecked accumulation of vast fortunes by billionaires distorts economies, deepens social inequality, and undermines democratic governance. As explored in previous chapters, extreme wealth concentration creates a host of societal problems, from environmental degradation to political corruption, and from labor exploitation to stagnating economic growth. These issues raise a critical question: Should there be a limit to how much wealth one individual can accumulate?

This chapter explores concrete policies that can be implemented to limit extreme wealth accumulation and redistribute resources more equitably. We will discuss the concept of a wealth cap, or wealth ceiling, which would impose a maximum threshold for individual wealth. This idea, though bold, is not entirely new; many historical and contemporary economic systems have recognized the dangers of excessive wealth concentration and taken steps to limit it. Here, we will outline a vision for a wealth ceiling and examine how it could be enforced through progressive taxation, inheritance taxes, capital gains reforms, and corporate restructuring. We will also explore incremental steps that can pave the way toward these more radical changes.

The Case for a Wealth Ceiling

Before diving into the specifics of how to implement a billionaire limit, it's important to understand the rationale behind such a policy. The fundamental argument for a wealth ceiling is based on the idea that extreme wealth concentration is inherently harmful to society. When a small group of people holds an overwhelming proportion of the world's wealth, it distorts the balance of power, undermines social cohesion, and perpetuates inequality.

Economically, extreme wealth accumulation often leads to inefficient allocation of resources. Billionaires tend to invest their wealth in low-risk, high-yield financial assets, rather than productive investments that create jobs or spur innovation. As wealth becomes concentrated in the hands of a few, it is effectively hoarded, contributing little to the broader economy. Furthermore, as discussed in previous chapters, the immense political influence wielded by billionaires allows them to shape policies in ways that protect their wealth and privilege, exacerbating inequality and limiting opportunities for others.

A wealth ceiling would address these issues by imposing a maximum limit on individual wealth. Any wealth accumulated beyond this threshold would be subject to heavy taxation or mandatory redistribution. The idea is not to punish success, but to ensure that wealth is shared more equitably and that no one individual or family has the power to accumulate such vast fortunes that they can dominate the economic, political, or social landscape.

Defining the Wealth Ceiling

One of the first challenges in implementing a wealth ceiling is determining the threshold at which it should be set. How much wealth is too much? Should the limit be set at $1 billion, $500 million, or some other figure? The answer to this question depends on several factors, including the goals of the policy, the economic context, and the level of inequality in society.

Some economists and political thinkers have proposed a wealth ceiling of $1 billion. This figure is symbolic, as it represents the point at which an individual's wealth exceeds any reasonable measure of personal or familial need. After all, $1 billion is an immense amount of money—enough to live in luxury for multiple lifetimes, even when accounting for future generations. Beyond this point, wealth accumulation serves little purpose other than to amass power and influence.

Others argue for a lower threshold, such as $500 million or even $100 million. These figures may seem less extreme, but they still represent more wealth than most people could spend in a lifetime. Lowering the threshold would allow for more substantial redistribution and could have a greater impact on reducing inequality. Ultimately, the exact figure for the wealth ceiling would need to be determined through a democratic process, taking into account the economic and social goals of the policy.

Progressive Taxation: The Key to Enforcing a Wealth Ceiling

Once a wealth ceiling has been established, the next step is determining how to enforce it. The most effective tool for limiting extreme wealth accumulation is a progressive taxation system. Progressive taxes impose higher rates on individuals and corporations as their income or wealth increases, ensuring that those who benefit the most from the economy contribute proportionally more to public resources.

While many countries already have progressive income tax systems, these are often riddled with loopholes and exemptions that allow the wealthy to avoid paying their fair share. To effectively enforce a wealth ceiling, these tax systems would need to be reformed and expanded to target not just income, but also wealth itself. Here are some key components of a progressive taxation system that could be used to enforce a billionaire limit:

Wealth Taxes

A wealth tax is a tax on an individual's total net worth, rather than just their annual income. This includes all assets, such as real estate, stocks, bonds, and business holdings. A wealth tax could be structured with progressively higher rates for larger fortunes. For example, wealth up to $50 million could be taxed at a relatively low rate, while wealth between $50 million and $1 billion could be taxed at a higher rate. Any wealth above the $1 billion threshold could be taxed at an even steeper rate, effectively functioning as a wealth ceiling.

Wealth taxes have been proposed by several prominent economists and politicians in recent years. In the United

States, Senator Elizabeth Warren and Senator Bernie Sanders have both proposed wealth taxes that would target the richest 0.1% of the population. Warren's plan, for example, would impose a 2% annual tax on wealth above $50 million, and a 6% tax on wealth above $1 billion. These proposals have gained significant public support, as they are seen as a way to curb extreme wealth concentration and fund vital public services.

One of the key advantages of a wealth tax is that it targets wealth that is often hidden from traditional income taxes. Billionaires typically accumulate much of their wealth in the form of capital gains, rather than income, allowing them to pay relatively low taxes. A wealth tax would ensure that all forms of wealth are subject to taxation, regardless of how they are earned.

Capital Gains Taxes

Another important tool for enforcing a wealth ceiling is reforming capital gains taxes. Capital gains are the profits earned from the sale of assets such as stocks, bonds, and real estate. In many countries, capital gains are taxed at lower rates than income, allowing wealthy individuals to accumulate large amounts of wealth without paying significant taxes.

To limit extreme wealth accumulation, capital gains taxes should be aligned with income tax rates, or even taxed at higher rates for very large gains. This would ensure that billionaires who derive much of their wealth from investments are taxed fairly, rather than being able to shelter their wealth in financial assets.

In addition, capital gains should be taxed on an annual basis, rather than only when assets are sold. This would prevent billionaires from avoiding taxes by holding onto their assets indefinitely, a strategy known as "buy, borrow, die." By taxing unrealized capital gains, governments could capture a portion of the wealth that is accumulating in financial markets, even if it has not yet been converted into income.

Inheritance Taxes

One of the main ways that wealth is perpetuated across generations is through inheritance. When billionaires pass their fortunes on to their children or grandchildren, they effectively create a permanent class of ultra-wealthy individuals who never have to work to earn their wealth. This perpetuates inequality and ensures that a small elite continues to dominate the economy and society.

To combat this, inheritance taxes should be significantly increased for large estates. While many countries already have inheritance taxes in place, these are often set at relatively low rates or apply only to very large estates. By raising the rates on inheritances above a certain threshold—say, $10 million—governments could prevent the perpetuation of extreme wealth across generations. In addition, loopholes that allow wealthy families to avoid inheritance taxes through trusts, foundations, or other legal structures should be closed.

Corporate Reforms

In addition to targeting individual wealth, it's important to address the corporate structures that allow billionaires to accumulate vast fortunes in the first place. Many billionaires derive their wealth from ownership of large corporations, which often operate in ways that prioritize profit maximization for shareholders over the welfare of workers, consumers, and the environment. To limit extreme wealth accumulation, corporate governance and taxation must be reformed to ensure that wealth is distributed more equitably within companies.

One approach is to implement policies that give workers a greater share of corporate profits. This could be achieved through employee ownership programs, profit-sharing schemes, or co-determination policies that give workers a voice in corporate decision-making. By redistributing profits more equitably within companies, these policies would help ensure that the wealth generated by businesses is shared among all those who contribute to their success, rather than being concentrated in the hands of a few billionaire owners.

In addition, corporate taxes should be reformed to ensure that large companies pay their fair share. Many multinational corporations use complex legal structures to avoid paying taxes in the countries where they operate, shifting profits to tax havens or exploiting loopholes in tax law. By closing these loopholes and imposing higher corporate tax rates on large companies, governments could reduce the accumulation of wealth by billionaire business owners and ensure that more of that wealth is reinvested in public goods.

Incremental Steps Toward a Wealth Ceiling

While the idea of a wealth ceiling may seem radical, it is possible to implement such a policy through incremental steps. Rather than immediately imposing a strict limit on individual wealth, governments can introduce a series of reforms that gradually move toward this goal. Here are some incremental steps that could pave the way for a wealth ceiling:

1. Strengthening Existing Progressive Taxes: Many countries already have progressive income taxes and capital gains taxes, but these systems often contain loopholes and exemptions that allow the wealthy to avoid paying their fair share. By closing these loopholes and raising tax rates on the highest earners, governments can begin to limit extreme wealth accumulation.

2. Introducing Wealth Taxes: While wealth taxes are not yet common, several countries have begun to explore this option. Implementing a modest wealth tax on fortunes above $50 million, for example, would be an important step toward capping extreme wealth.

3. Increasing Inheritance Taxes: Inheritance taxes are a key tool for preventing the perpetuation of wealth across generations. By raising the rates on large estates and closing loopholes, governments can ensure that wealth is redistributed more equitably.

4. Corporate Reforms: Implementing policies that give workers a greater share of corporate profits and closing corporate tax loopholes would help limit the wealth accumulation of billionaire business owners and ensure that companies contribute more to the broader economy.

5. Public Campaigns and Education: Building public support for a wealth ceiling is essential for its successful implementation. Governments, activists, and academics can work together to raise awareness of the dangers of extreme wealth concentration and build a movement for progressive taxation and wealth redistribution.

The Path to a Fairer Society

The idea of a billionaire limit is not about punishing success or demonizing the wealthy. Rather, it is about creating a fairer, more equitable society in which wealth is distributed more justly, and the immense power that comes with extreme wealth is curtailed. By implementing progressive taxation, wealth taxes, inheritance taxes, and corporate reforms, governments can begin to limit the accumulation of vast fortunes and ensure that resources are reinvested in public goods and services that benefit all citizens.

The path to a wealth ceiling may not be easy, but it is a necessary step if we are to address the deep inequalities that plague our societies. By setting a limit on extreme wealth, we can create a more just and sustainable economy that works for everyone, not just the billionaire elite.

Chapter 11: Redistribution Strategies

In a society where extreme wealth accumulation has been curtailed, the next logical step is to figure out how to redistribute that excess wealth in ways that benefit the broader population. Simply capping individual wealth or taxing billionaires more heavily is not enough. The real challenge lies in determining the best strategies for utilizing those resources to create a more equitable, prosperous, and sustainable society.

Redistributing wealth isn't just about addressing the moral and ethical problems associated with inequality; it's also a practical solution to many of the most pressing issues facing society today, such as poverty, lack of access to education and healthcare, housing shortages, and deteriorating infrastructure. The resources that currently sit in the coffers of a few billionaires could instead be used to bolster the social safety net, fund critical public services, and invest in long-term projects that benefit everyone.

This chapter explores various strategies for redistributing wealth, focusing on policies like universal basic income (UBI), free education and healthcare, public housing initiatives, and infrastructure investments. Each of these policies addresses a key area where inequality manifests itself and where concentrated wealth could be most effectively deployed to improve quality of life for the majority of people. The overarching argument is that redistributing wealth isn't just about charity—it's about building a more resilient, fair, and dynamic economy that works for everyone, not just the wealthiest few.

The Rationale for Redistribution

Before digging into specific strategies, it's important to address the fundamental question: Why redistribute wealth in the first place? The argument for wealth redistribution is rooted in both moral and economic principles.

On a moral level, extreme wealth inequality is inherently unjust. In a world where billions of people struggle to meet basic needs, while a small handful of individuals amass fortunes that exceed the GDP of entire nations, the imbalance is stark. This inequality exacerbates social problems like poverty, crime, and poor health outcomes, and it undermines the sense of social cohesion necessary for a functioning democracy.

Economically, wealth redistribution is a way to correct market failures that arise from excessive concentration of resources. When wealth is concentrated in the hands of a few, it tends to be hoarded or invested in ways that primarily benefit the wealthy themselves, such as luxury goods, real estate speculation, or financial markets. This does little to stimulate the broader economy or create jobs. In contrast, when wealth is redistributed to lower- and middle-income individuals, it is more likely to be spent on goods and services, thereby increasing demand, boosting economic growth, and creating a more vibrant and sustainable economy.

With these rationales in mind, let's explore some of the most effective ways to redistribute wealth.

Universal Basic Income (UBI)

One of the most widely discussed strategies for wealth redistribution is universal basic income (UBI). UBI is a system in which every citizen receives a regular, unconditional payment from the government, regardless of their employment status or income level. The idea behind UBI is to provide a financial floor that ensures everyone has access to the basic necessities of life, such as food, shelter, and healthcare.

The Case for UBI

Proponents of UBI argue that it is an effective way to combat poverty, reduce inequality, and provide economic security in an increasingly automated world. As automation and artificial intelligence (AI) displace jobs in industries ranging from manufacturing to services, many workers face the prospect of long-term unemployment or underemployment. UBI offers a solution by providing a guaranteed income that allows people to meet their basic needs even if traditional employment becomes less available.

UBI also has the advantage of being simple and efficient to administer. Unlike many social welfare programs that require extensive means testing, bureaucracy, and administrative overhead, UBI is a straightforward payment to all citizens. This reduces the stigma often associated with welfare programs and ensures that no one falls through the cracks.

Furthermore, UBI can serve as a powerful economic stimulus. When people have more money in their pockets, they are likely to spend it on goods and services, boosting demand and driving economic growth. This is particularly true for lower-income individuals, who tend to spend a higher proportion of their income on necessities, thereby circulating money more quickly through the economy.

Funding UBI Through Wealth Redistribution

Implementing UBI on a large scale requires significant financial resources, which is where wealth redistribution comes into play. The excess wealth accumulated by billionaires and large corporations can be redirected to fund UBI payments for the entire population. Progressive taxation, wealth taxes, and capital gains reforms, as discussed in previous chapters, can generate the necessary revenue to support a robust UBI program.

Countries like Finland and Canada have already experimented with UBI pilot programs, showing promising results in terms of poverty reduction and overall well-being. By redistributing wealth through UBI, governments can create a more stable and secure economy, where people have the freedom to pursue education, entrepreneurship, or caregiving without the constant fear of financial instability.

Free Education and Healthcare

Another critical area for wealth redistribution is the provision of free, high-quality education and healthcare. Access to these essential services is a fundamental human right, yet in many countries, particularly the United States, education and healthcare are treated as commodities that individuals must purchase. This creates a two-tiered system where the wealthy can afford the best services, while the poor are left with substandard options or none at all.

Education as a Public Good

Education is one of the most powerful tools for reducing inequality and promoting social mobility. However, in many parts of the world, access to quality education is limited by one's economic background. Wealthy families can afford private schools, tutors, and higher education, while low-income families often struggle to afford even the most basic educational resources.

By redistributing wealth to fund free, universal education, governments can level the playing field and ensure that every child has the opportunity to succeed, regardless of their family's income. This includes not only primary and secondary education but also higher education, which has become prohibitively expensive for many. Free college and vocational training programs can help bridge the skills gap and prepare workers for the jobs of the future, particularly as automation and technological change reshape the labor market.

Countries like Norway, Finland, and Germany have already demonstrated that free, high-quality education is both feasible and beneficial. These countries have some of the highest literacy rates, college graduation rates, and levels of social mobility in the world. Their education systems are funded through progressive taxation, which ensures that the wealthy contribute a fair share toward the public good.

Healthcare for All

Like education, healthcare is a basic necessity that should not be dependent on one's ability to pay. In countries with privatized healthcare systems, millions of people lack access to necessary medical treatments, leading to preventable deaths, poor health outcomes, and financial ruin. The COVID-19 pandemic highlighted the dangers of an unequal healthcare system, as marginalized communities suffered disproportionately from the virus due to lack of access to healthcare.

A publicly funded, universal healthcare system ensures that everyone receives the care they need, regardless of income. Wealth redistribution can provide the resources necessary to create such a system, reducing the burden on individuals and families who are currently forced to pay out of pocket for medical expenses or rely on inadequate insurance coverage.

Countries with universal healthcare, such as the United Kingdom, Canada, and Sweden, have shown that it is possible to provide high-quality healthcare to all citizens without bankrupting the government. These systems are funded through progressive taxation, ensuring that the wealthiest individuals contribute the most to the public health system. By redistributing wealth in this way, societies can improve health outcomes, reduce inequality, and create a more resilient healthcare infrastructure.

Public Housing Initiatives

Another key area where wealth redistribution can have a transformative impact is housing. The housing crisis in many cities around the world has reached alarming levels, with skyrocketing rents and home prices pushing millions of people into homelessness or forcing them to live in substandard conditions. Meanwhile, real estate developers and wealthy investors profit from the housing market, often driving gentrification and displacement.

The Need for Affordable Housing

Access to safe, affordable housing is a basic human right, yet it is increasingly out of reach for many. In cities like San Francisco, New York, London, and Paris, the cost of living has risen so dramatically that even middle-income families struggle to afford rent, let alone buy a home. This exacerbates inequality, as the wealthy can continue to accumulate assets through real estate investment, while the poor are forced into precarious housing situations.

Redistributing wealth to fund public housing initiatives can help address this crisis. Governments can use the revenue generated from wealth taxes and other forms of progressive taxation to build affordable housing units, renovate existing public housing, and provide subsidies to low-income families. This would not only reduce homelessness but also provide economic stability for millions of people who currently spend a disproportionate share of their income on housing.

Models for Success

Several cities and countries have already implemented successful public housing programs that can serve as models for broader wealth redistribution efforts. In Vienna, Austria, for example, nearly 60% of the population lives in municipally owned or subsidized housing. The city has made a long-term commitment to affordable housing, funding it through a combination of public investment and taxes on real estate speculation. As a result, Vienna has one of the lowest rates of homelessness in Europe and is consistently ranked as one of the most livable cities in the world.

Similarly, Singapore has created a robust public housing system where over 80% of residents live in government-built flats. These flats are sold at subsidized rates to citizens, and the government ensures that housing remains affordable through strict regulations on resale and speculation. By prioritizing public housing, Singapore has managed to avoid the extreme housing inequality seen in many other global cities.

Redistributing wealth to fund public housing initiatives not only addresses the immediate problem of housing insecurity but also has long-term benefits for social mobility, health, and economic stability.

Infrastructure Investments

Infrastructure is the backbone of any economy, yet in many countries, particularly in the Global North, public infrastructure has been allowed to deteriorate due to lack of investment. Roads, bridges, public transportation, water systems, and energy grids are all essential for the functioning of society, yet they are often neglected in favor of tax cuts for the wealthy or military spending.

Redistributing wealth to fund infrastructure investments can have a profound impact on economic growth, job creation, and quality of life. Modernizing infrastructure not only improves efficiency and productivity but also creates millions of jobs in construction, engineering, and related industries.

Building a More Equitable Future

Wealth redistribution is not about punishing the wealthy; it's about building a more equitable, sustainable future where everyone has access to the resources they need to thrive. By implementing strategies like universal basic income, free education and healthcare, public housing initiatives, and infrastructure investments, governments can create a society where wealth is shared more broadly and used to benefit the many, not just the few.

These redistribution strategies are not utopian fantasies but practical solutions that have been successfully implemented in various forms around the world. The key is to build political will and public support for policies that prioritize the common good over the accumulation of private wealth. In doing so, we can create a more just and prosperous world for future generations.

Chapter 12: The Role of Government and Regulation

The role of government is central to enforcing wealth caps and ensuring the fair distribution of resources in society. Without strong governmental action, the policies and strategies discussed throughout this book, such as wealth redistribution, wealth limits, and corporate reform, would remain theoretical rather than practical solutions to the problem of extreme wealth inequality. Governments, by nature, have the power to create laws, enforce regulations, and ensure that the public interest is prioritized over private gain. This chapter will explore how governments can use their authority to curtail the influence of billionaires and ensure a more equitable distribution of resources.

Governments, however, must also contend with the immense power and influence that billionaires currently hold over political processes and economic systems. Billionaires, through lobbying, political donations, and control of media, often exert outsized influence on governments, shaping policies in their favor. This chapter will therefore also explore how to break the cycle of billionaire influence over politics, and the importance of building robust democratic institutions that are resistant to the undue power of wealth.

Additionally, in today's globalized economy, it is not enough for individual governments to act in isolation. Billionaires often exploit the international nature of finance to protect their wealth from national regulations, using tax havens, offshore accounts, and global investment strategies to evade taxes and other regulations. International cooperation will be essential in enforcing wealth limits and ensuring that billionaires cannot easily shift their assets to avoid paying their fair share.

The Role of Government in Wealth Caps and Redistribution

Governments are the only institutions with the power to create and enforce laws that can effectively limit the accumulation of extreme wealth. In a democratic society, government power should be wielded in the service of the public good, ensuring that resources are distributed fairly and that no one individual or corporation can wield disproportionate influence over the economy or politics.

Legislative Measures for Wealth Caps

The primary tool that governments can use to limit the accumulation of extreme wealth is progressive taxation. As discussed in previous chapters, progressive taxes on income, capital gains, inheritance, and wealth can prevent individuals and corporations from accumulating vast fortunes. However, for progressive taxation to be effective, governments must also close the loopholes that the wealthy often exploit to avoid paying taxes.

Wealth Taxes: Implementing a wealth tax would directly target the accumulated assets of the ultra-wealthy, including stocks, bonds, real estate, art, and other forms of wealth. Wealth taxes would be applied annually, with higher rates for those who hold more wealth. A wealth tax would prevent the accumulation of extreme wealth over time, and ensure that billionaires contribute to public goods and services.

For example, a wealth tax of 2% on fortunes above $50 million, and a higher rate of 5% on fortunes over $1 billion, could generate significant revenue to be used for social programs like healthcare, education, and infrastructure. This approach was popularized by economists like Thomas Piketty, and has been proposed in the political arena by figures like U.S. Senator Elizabeth Warren.

Income and Capital Gains Taxes: Progressive income taxes, where the wealthiest individuals pay a higher percentage of their income in taxes, are a foundational tool for limiting wealth accumulation. Similarly, taxing capital gains—the profits from selling stocks, real estate, or other investments—at the same or higher rates than earned income would prevent billionaires from benefiting disproportionately from investments, while working individuals pay higher rates on their labor.

Inheritance and Estate Taxes: Another important aspect of wealth caps is inheritance and estate taxes. Wealth often perpetuates across generations, allowing the children of billionaires to inherit vast fortunes without contributing to the economy. High inheritance taxes on large estates would prevent this dynastic accumulation of wealth and ensure that more of the money is returned to the public.

Corporate Regulation

Corporate regulation is another critical area where governments must act to prevent billionaires from accumulating extreme wealth. Much of the wealth held by billionaires comes from ownership of corporations, and the practices of those corporations are often harmful to workers, consumers, and the environment. Governments must therefore implement regulations that ensure corporations act in the public interest and do not allow their owners to hoard wealth at the expense of society.

Profit-Sharing and Worker Representation: One way to limit the concentration of wealth among corporate owners is to implement policies that give workers a greater share of corporate profits and decision-making power. Employee stock ownership plans (ESOPs), profit-sharing arrangements, and worker representation on corporate boards would ensure that the benefits of corporate success are more widely distributed among workers, rather than concentrated in the hands of a few executives and shareholders.

Anti-Monopoly Laws: Strengthening anti-monopoly laws is essential to preventing the creation of corporate empires that dominate entire industries and allow their owners to amass vast fortunes. In the tech industry, for example, companies like Amazon, Google, and Facebook have grown to monopolize key areas of the digital economy, stifling competition and allowing their founders to accumulate unprecedented wealth. Governments must enforce existing antitrust laws and pass new legislation to break up monopolies and promote competition.

Closing Tax Loopholes for Corporations: Many billionaires use their corporations to avoid paying taxes by exploiting loopholes in the tax code. For example, some large corporations report profits in low-tax countries or offshore accounts, even though most of their business is conducted in high-tax countries. Governments must close these loopholes and ensure that corporations pay taxes based on where their economic activity takes place.

Breaking the Cycle of Billionaire Influence in Politics

One of the greatest challenges in regulating billionaires and curbing extreme wealth is the outsized influence that billionaires wield over political processes. Through campaign contributions, lobbying efforts, and control of media outlets, billionaires have shaped policies in ways that protect their wealth and entrench inequality. For example, billionaires have lobbied for lower corporate tax rates, weaker labor protections, and deregulation of industries where they hold major stakes.

Governments must take steps to reduce the influence of billionaires in politics and ensure that the democratic process represents the will of the people, not just the interests of the wealthy elite.

Campaign Finance Reform

One of the primary ways billionaires exert influence over politics is through campaign contributions. In countries like the United States, political campaigns are increasingly reliant on large donations from wealthy individuals and corporations.

This gives billionaires enormous power to shape the political agenda by supporting candidates who prioritize their interests.

Campaign finance reform is essential to reducing billionaire influence in politics. Governments should implement strict limits on campaign contributions, ensuring that political candidates are not beholden to wealthy donors. Publicly funded elections, where candidates receive government funding rather than private donations, would create a more level playing field and reduce the influence of money in politics.

Lobbying Restrictions

Lobbying is another key avenue through which billionaires and corporations influence government policy. Billionaires often hire armies of lobbyists to push for policies that benefit their businesses, such as tax cuts, deregulation, and subsidies. Lobbyists also write legislation, meet with lawmakers, and work behind the scenes to ensure that the interests of the wealthy are prioritized over the needs of ordinary citizens.

To curb the influence of lobbying, governments should implement strict transparency and accountability measures. Lobbyists should be required to disclose their activities, including the legislation they influence and the money they spend. Additionally, governments should enact cooling-off periods that prevent former lawmakers and government officials from immediately becoming lobbyists after leaving office.

Media Ownership and Influence

Billionaires also exert power over public opinion through ownership of media outlets. Controlling the media allows billionaires to shape the narrative around key political and economic issues, ensuring that their interests are represented favorably in the public sphere. For example, billionaires who own major newspapers, television stations, or social media platforms can influence coverage of issues like taxation, regulation, and labor rights.

To counteract the concentration of media ownership, governments should enforce anti-monopoly laws in the media industry and promote diverse ownership of media outlets. Public funding for independent journalism and nonprofit media organizations would also help ensure that a wide range of voices and perspectives are represented in the media, rather than allowing billionaires to dominate the discourse.

International Cooperation to Combat Tax Havens and Offshore Accounts

One of the biggest challenges in regulating billionaire wealth in the modern world is the global nature of finance. Billionaires can move their assets across borders with ease, using tax havens, offshore accounts, and shell companies to evade taxes and hide their wealth from government regulators. Without international cooperation, efforts to limit wealth accumulation and redistribute resources will be undermined by the ability of the wealthy to simply move their money to jurisdictions with lower taxes and fewer regulations.

The Problem of Tax Havens

Tax havens are countries or territories that offer low or no taxes on income, capital gains, or wealth, and provide secrecy for individuals and corporations looking to hide their assets. Many of the world's billionaires use tax havens to avoid paying taxes in their home countries, shifting profits and wealth to places like the Cayman Islands, Luxembourg, or Switzerland.

For example, the "Panama Papers" and "Paradise Papers" leaks revealed how the world's wealthiest individuals and corporations use complex networks of offshore accounts and shell companies to hide their wealth and avoid paying taxes. This system of global tax evasion deprives governments of the revenue needed to fund public services, and allows billionaires to accumulate wealth unchecked.

The Need for International Cooperation

To effectively combat tax evasion and wealth hiding, governments must work together on an international level. Global cooperation is essential to closing tax loopholes, sharing information about financial accounts, and enforcing laws against tax evasion. Several international organizations, such as the Organisation for Economic Co-operation and Development (OECD), have already begun to address these issues by promoting transparency and information-sharing between countries.

One important initiative is the OECD's Common Reporting Standard (CRS), which requires countries to automatically exchange information about financial accounts held by non-residents. This makes it harder for billionaires to hide their wealth in offshore accounts without being detected by their home country's tax authorities.

Governments should also collaborate to implement a global minimum tax on corporations, ensuring that businesses cannot avoid taxes by shifting profits to low-tax jurisdictions. A global minimum tax would prevent a "race to the bottom," where countries compete to offer the lowest tax rates to attract investment from multinational corporations.

Strengthening Anti-Trust Laws and Labor Rights Protections

In addition to tax policies and political reforms, governments must also focus on strengthening anti-trust laws and labor rights protections to reduce the power of billionaires and promote a more equitable economy.

Anti-Trust Enforcement

As discussed earlier in this chapter, monopolies and corporate consolidation allow billionaires to accumulate vast fortunes by stifling competition and controlling entire industries. Governments must strengthen anti-trust laws and actively enforce them to break up monopolies and promote competition.

For example, tech giants like Amazon, Google, and Facebook have been accused of using their market dominance to squash competitors, exploit workers, and amass enormous wealth. Governments should use anti-trust laws to break up these companies, promote competition, and ensure that no single corporation or individual holds too much power in the economy.

Strengthening Labor Rights

Finally, governments must also strengthen labor rights protections to ensure that workers are paid fairly and treated with dignity. Billionaires often accumulate their wealth by exploiting workers, paying low wages, and resisting unionization efforts. By enacting strong labor laws, governments can ensure that workers have the power to negotiate for better wages and working conditions.

Policies such as raising the minimum wage, protecting the right to unionize, and enforcing workplace safety standards would prevent billionaires from profiting at the expense of workers. Additionally, governments should promote policies that ensure workers have a share in corporate profits, such as employee stock ownership plans and profit-sharing arrangements.

The Role of Government in Building a More Equitable Society

The role of government in regulating billionaires and ensuring the fair distribution of resources is essential to building a more equitable society. By implementing progressive taxation, closing tax loopholes, strengthening anti-trust laws, and promoting labor rights, governments can prevent the accumulation of extreme wealth and promote the public good. International cooperation is also crucial to combating tax evasion and ensuring that billionaires cannot hide their wealth in offshore accounts.

At the same time, governments must break the cycle of billionaire influence in politics by enacting campaign finance reforms, restricting lobbying, and promoting diverse media ownership. Only by curbing the power of wealth in politics can governments truly represent the interests of the people, rather than the interests of the ultra-wealthy.

Ultimately, government action is key to creating a society where wealth is distributed fairly and everyone has the opportunity to thrive. By using the tools of legislation, regulation, and international cooperation, governments can build a future where the concentration of wealth in the hands of a few is replaced by a more just and equitable economy for all.

Chapter 13: Social Movements and Grassroots Organizing

While governments play a critical role in implementing laws and regulations to address wealth inequality, history has shown that political will alone is rarely enough to drive significant change. Power dynamics are deeply entrenched in systems that benefit the ultra-wealthy, and those who hold immense wealth and influence are often resistant to any policies that might curtail their dominance. This is where social movements and grassroots organizing become essential. The push for wealth redistribution, fair labor practices, and curbing the influence of billionaires requires sustained public pressure, which can only be achieved through organized movements that represent the interests of the broader population.

This chapter explores the vital role of social movements in fostering political change, particularly in curbing the accumulation of wealth and power by billionaires. It examines how unions, advocacy groups, and grassroots organizations have historically played a pivotal role in driving systemic change. It also analyzes contemporary movements pushing for reforms today and how these groups can influence policy in the future. Lastly, the chapter provides lessons from past successful movements, offering a blueprint for how society can build momentum to challenge the unchecked power of the ultra-wealthy.

The Role of Social Movements in Driving Change

Social movements are collective efforts by large groups of people who aim to bring about social, political, or economic change. These movements often emerge from dissatisfaction with the status quo and represent voices that are marginalized or ignored by mainstream political and economic systems. They challenge the existing power structures and demand reforms that align with principles of equity, justice, and fairness.

One of the fundamental advantages of social movements is their ability to organize and mobilize people across different sectors of society, creating a unified force that can demand change from governments and other institutions. By amplifying public awareness and channeling collective action, social movements can exert pressure on political leaders to enact reforms, even in the face of resistance from powerful economic elites.

Historically, social movements have been instrumental in addressing a wide range of issues, from labor rights to civil rights, environmental protection, gender equality, and more. In the context of limiting billionaire wealth and redistributing resources, these movements must focus on addressing the root causes of economic inequality, demanding stronger labor protections, fair taxation, and corporate accountability.

Unions and Labor Movements

One of the most significant and enduring forms of grassroots organizing has been the labor movement, which has played a central role in challenging the concentration of wealth and power in the hands of a few. Throughout history, unions and labor organizations have fought to improve wages, working conditions, and job security for workers. They have also played a key role in reducing the power disparity between workers and wealthy business owners by advocating for collective bargaining, fair labor laws, and worker representation in decision-making processes.

The Rise of Labor Unions

The rise of labor unions in the late 19th and early 20th centuries was a direct response to the exploitation of workers by wealthy industrialists during the Gilded Age. At that time, many factory owners and business magnates accumulated immense wealth through low wages, long working hours, and unsafe working conditions. Workers were seen as disposable, and the immense profits generated by their labor went almost entirely to the owners of capital.

Labor unions emerged as a form of collective resistance, uniting workers to demand better treatment and fair compensation. Unions used a variety of tactics, including strikes, boycotts, and negotiations, to put pressure on business owners and the government. One of the most famous examples of this was the 1912 Lawrence Textile Strike, led by the Industrial Workers of the World (IWW), where thousands of immigrant workers organized against wage cuts. The strike was successful, and it led to wage increases not just in Lawrence, Massachusetts, but across the industry.

Labor unions were also instrumental in securing the passage of critical labor laws, such as the Fair Labor Standards Act in the United States, which established a minimum wage, overtime pay, and restrictions on child labor. These victories were hard-fought and often met with violent opposition from business owners and government forces. However, through sustained organizing and public pressure, unions were able to force the hand of the political establishment, leading to significant improvements in workers' rights and a reduction in wealth inequality.

The Decline of Unions and the Rise of Billionaire Power

Despite their historical successes, unions have faced significant challenges in recent decades, particularly in countries like the United States, where union membership has been in decline since the 1980s. This decline has coincided with the rise of neoliberal economic policies, which emphasize deregulation, privatization, and free markets. These policies have often favored the interests of corporations and the wealthy, leading to increased economic inequality and the consolidation of billionaire power.

The decline of unions has also been driven by aggressive anti-union tactics by corporations, such as union-busting, outsourcing, and the increased use of precarious employment contracts. Without the counterbalance of strong labor movements, workers have been left vulnerable to exploitation, and the wealth generated by their labor has flowed increasingly to the top, contributing to the rise of billionaires.

The weakening of unions has had a profound impact on wealth distribution. Without the ability to collectively bargain for better wages and working conditions, workers have seen their share of national income decline, while corporate profits and CEO pay have skyrocketed. This has created a widening gap between the ultra-wealthy and the rest of society.

Rebuilding Labor Movements for the 21st Century

In order to address the growing power of billionaires and restore economic balance, it is essential to rebuild labor movements for the 21st century. This will require unions to adapt to new economic realities, such as globalization, automation, and the rise of the gig economy, where traditional forms of employment are being replaced by short-term, precarious work arrangements.

One promising avenue for rebuilding labor movements is through organizing in sectors that have historically been difficult to unionize, such as the tech industry, gig work, and service industries. In recent years, there have been notable efforts to unionize workers at companies like Amazon, Google, and Uber, where billionaires like Jeff Bezos have amassed enormous fortunes while workers face low wages, grueling working conditions, and limited benefits.

Another important strategy is to build international solidarity among workers. In a globalized economy, where corporations can easily move jobs and production to countries with lower labor standards, it is crucial for labor movements to work across borders to demand fair treatment for workers everywhere. Global labor organizations, such as the International Trade Union Confederation (ITUC), play a key role in coordinating efforts to improve labor standards worldwide.

By revitalizing labor movements and adapting to new economic realities, workers can reclaim their power and challenge the concentration of wealth in the hands of billionaires. Strong labor movements are essential to creating a more equitable economy, where the wealth generated by labor is shared more fairly among workers and not hoarded by a few at the top.

Advocacy Groups and Grassroots Organizing

In addition to labor unions, a wide range of advocacy groups and grassroots organizations play a vital role in raising awareness about wealth inequality and pushing for reforms. These groups often focus on specific issues related to economic justice, such as tax reform, corporate accountability, environmental sustainability, and social safety nets. They work to mobilize public opinion, influence policymakers, and build coalitions that can drive systemic change.

The Role of Advocacy Groups in Raising Awareness

Advocacy groups are often at the forefront of raising public awareness about the harmful effects of wealth inequality and the need for reforms. Through research, media campaigns, and public education efforts, these groups help to highlight the ways in which the concentration of wealth among billionaires undermines democracy, exacerbates social problems, and contributes to economic instability.

For example, organizations like Oxfam and the Institute for Policy Studies have been instrumental in bringing attention to the issue of wealth inequality on a global scale. Oxfam's annual reports on global inequality have shown how the wealth of billionaires continues to grow at an alarming rate, while millions of people around the world struggle to meet basic needs like food, housing, and healthcare. By shining a spotlight on these issues, advocacy groups help to shift public opinion and build support for policies that limit extreme wealth.

Grassroots Organizing and Building Public Pressure

Grassroots organizing is a key strategy for building public pressure and mobilizing people to demand change. Grassroots movements are often decentralized, with local communities organizing around issues that directly affect them. These movements rely on the participation of ordinary citizens, who take collective action through protests, petitions, town hall meetings, and other forms of activism.

One of the most powerful examples of grassroots organizing in recent history is the Occupy Wall Street movement, which emerged in 2011 as a response to the growing concentration of wealth and power among the "1%"—a term used to describe the wealthiest individuals and corporations. Occupy Wall Street began as a protest in New York City's financial district, but quickly grew into a global movement, with people in cities around the world taking to the streets to demand economic justice.

Although the Occupy movement did not achieve all of its goals, it succeeded in bringing the issue of wealth inequality to the forefront of public discourse. The movement popularized the slogan "We are the 99%," highlighting the stark divide between the wealthy elite and the rest of society. Occupy Wall Street also inspired a new generation of activists and laid the groundwork for future movements focused on economic justice.

Coalitions for Change: Building Alliances

To create lasting change, it is essential for advocacy groups and grassroots organizations to build broad coalitions that bring together diverse constituencies. Wealth inequality affects many different groups in society, including workers, students, retirees, people of color, and women, among others. By building alliances across these groups, social movements can create a powerful force for change that is difficult for political leaders to ignore.

One example of successful coalition-building is the **Fight for $15** movement, which has brought together low-wage workers, labor unions, and community organizations to demand a $15 minimum wage and better working conditions. The movement began with fast-food workers in the United States, but quickly spread to other sectors and cities. Through strikes, protests, and advocacy, the Fight for $15 has succeeded in raising the minimum wage in several U.S. states and cities, and has sparked similar movements around the world.

Lessons from Successful Social Movements

History is filled with examples of social movements that have successfully challenged entrenched power structures and brought about significant social, political, and economic reforms. By studying these movements, we can learn valuable lessons about how to build and sustain momentum for change.

The Civil Rights Movement

One of the most iconic social movements of the 20th century is the Civil Rights Movement in the United States. Led by figures like Martin Luther King Jr., Rosa Parks, and Malcolm X, the Civil Rights Movement fought to end racial segregation and discrimination against African Americans. Through nonviolent protests, civil disobedience, and legal challenges, the movement succeeded in securing landmark legislation, such as the Civil Rights Act of 1964 and the Voting Rights Act of 1965.

The success of the Civil Rights Movement was due in large part to its ability to build broad coalitions and mobilize large numbers of people. The movement brought together activists from diverse backgrounds, including religious leaders, students, labor unions, and civil rights organizations. It also used media effectively to raise awareness and gain public support for its cause.

The Civil Rights Movement offers important lessons for contemporary movements focused on economic justice. Like the Civil Rights Movement, today's social movements must build broad coalitions, use media to raise awareness, and employ a variety of tactics to pressure political leaders to act.

The Women's Suffrage Movement

Another successful social movement is the Women's Suffrage Movement, which fought for women's right to vote. The movement began in the mid-19th century and culminated in the passage of the 19th Amendment to the U.S. Constitution in 1920, which granted women the right to vote.

The Women's Suffrage Movement faced significant opposition from political leaders and society at large, but it persisted through decades of organizing, protests, and advocacy. Like the Civil Rights Movement, the Women's Suffrage Movement succeeded by building broad coalitions and mobilizing large numbers of people. It also used creative tactics, such as public demonstrations, parades, and lobbying efforts, to raise awareness and build support for its cause.

The Women's Suffrage Movement is a reminder that social change often takes time, and that persistence and determination are key to success. Today's movements for economic justice must be prepared for a long struggle, but history shows that sustained organizing and activism can lead to significant reforms.

The Power of People to Challenge Billionaire Wealth

In the face of growing wealth inequality and the concentration of power in the hands of billionaires, social movements and grassroots organizing offer a path forward. Through unions, advocacy groups, and broad-based coalitions, ordinary people can come together to demand change and push for policies that limit extreme wealth, redistribute resources, and build a more equitable society.

While political leaders may be reluctant to take on the power of billionaires, history has shown that sustained public pressure can lead to significant reforms. Whether through strikes, protests, lobbying efforts, or media campaigns, social movements have the power to challenge the status quo and create a more just and fair economy.

Ultimately, the fight against billionaire wealth is not just about economic policy—it is about the fundamental principles of democracy, fairness, and social justice. By organizing and mobilizing, people can reclaim their power and build a society where wealth is shared more equitably and everyone has the opportunity to thrive.

Chapter 14: Building a Post-Billionaire Economy

In the previous chapters, we have discussed the immense concentration of wealth in the hands of a few, the moral and economic implications of billionaire wealth, and strategies for redistributing wealth and limiting excessive accumulation. But what comes after? What would a society look like without billionaires? How would it function, and what would the economic, social, and political structures look like? This chapter delves into the vision of a post-billionaire economy—one that prioritizes collective well-being over individual wealth, emphasizes equitable distribution of resources, and fosters sustainability and democratic governance over profit-driven exploitation.

By removing the distortions that billionaire wealth introduces into the system, a post-billionaire economy could fundamentally reshape how we think about work, capital, and the purpose of economic activity. Such an economy would not only redistribute wealth but also reform the structures of business and governance to create a more sustainable, just, and inclusive world.

1. Prioritizing Collective Well-Being

A post-billionaire economy would place collective well-being—rather than individual accumulation of wealth—at the center of its ethos. In this paradigm, the success of an economy is not measured by how many billionaires it can produce or how much wealth can be concentrated in the hands of a few, but by how well it meets the needs of the broader population. This includes providing basic necessities like food, housing, healthcare, education, and clean energy to everyone, not as luxuries but as fundamental rights.

A Shift in Values

The concept of collective well-being contrasts sharply with the dominant economic narrative of our time, which values the pursuit of individual wealth, competition, and consumption. A society without billionaires would require a significant cultural shift, one that moves away from glorifying extreme wealth and consumption and instead values equity, sustainability, and community. In this framework, individual success is not measured solely by material wealth or financial standing but by how much one contributes to the collective good.

This shift in values would also promote the idea that human well-being extends beyond material wealth. Mental health, social connections, environmental quality, and personal fulfillment become key metrics for measuring the success of a post-billionaire economy. Wealth accumulation would be secondary to improving these other forms of well-being, ensuring that economic activities are aligned with human flourishing rather than profit maximization.

Universal Basic Services

In a post-billionaire economy, the state and society would focus on providing universal basic services—publicly funded and universally accessible services that ensure a minimum standard of living for all citizens. This could include healthcare, education, housing, transportation, and access to information. Universal basic services shift the responsibility for meeting basic needs away from market-driven solutions, where access to these services is based on individual wealth, and toward a system in which everyone has guaranteed access, regardless of income or social standing.

This model of public provisioning would also help reduce the need for excessive wealth accumulation by individuals, as people would no longer need to hoard resources to secure their access to healthcare, housing, and education. Instead, these would be seen as fundamental human rights, with the economy organized around providing them as efficiently and equitably as possible. Governments would redirect their focus toward creating well-functioning public systems that prioritize long-term societal needs over short-term profits.

2. A More Equitable Distribution of Resources

One of the central features of a post-billionaire economy would be the more equitable distribution of resources across society. Wealth would no longer be concentrated in the hands of a few individuals or corporations but would be distributed more evenly to ensure that everyone can meet their basic needs and have the opportunity to contribute to society.

Progressive Taxation

A post-billionaire economy would rely on progressive taxation to prevent wealth from accumulating excessively in the hands of individuals and corporations. Progressive taxation—where higher earners pay a higher percentage of their income in taxes—can ensure that the wealthiest contribute their fair share to society. This revenue can then be redistributed to fund social programs, public infrastructure, and universal services.

In this model, wealth caps or maximum income limits could be imposed to prevent individuals from amassing fortunes that would allow them to wield undue influence over politics, media, and the economy. By setting a ceiling on wealth, society could ensure that no individual accumulates more than is necessary for a comfortable life, while excess wealth is redirected to the public good.

Reclaiming the Commons

A more equitable distribution of resources would also involve reclaiming the commons—resources that should be collectively owned and managed for the benefit of all, rather than privatized for individual profit. This includes natural resources like water, air, and forests, as well as public infrastructure, healthcare systems, and education. In a post-billionaire economy, the commons would be protected from exploitation by private interests and managed in a way that prioritizes sustainability and long-term public welfare.

This would mean reversing trends of privatization, where public assets are sold off to private corporations that then extract profits while providing poorer services. Instead, these resources would remain under public ownership and democratic control, ensuring they are used for the benefit of all rather than for the enrichment of a few.

3. Restructuring Businesses and Industries

A key component of the post-billionaire economy is the restructuring of businesses and industries to prioritize workers, communities, and the environment over short-term profits. The current model of corporate governance, where companies are beholden to maximizing shareholder value above all else, has led to a system in which wealth accumulates at the top while workers and the environment are exploited. A new model is needed—one that aligns business operations with the needs of society and the planet.

Worker Ownership and Cooperatives

One of the most effective ways to democratize wealth and ensure that businesses serve the public good is through worker ownership and cooperatives. In these models, businesses are owned and managed by the workers themselves, rather than by distant shareholders or billionaire owners. This gives workers a direct stake in the success of the company, as well as a voice in decision-making processes.

Worker cooperatives are structured around principles of democracy, where each worker has an equal vote in how the business is run, regardless of their position or level of investment. This ensures that decisions are made with the well-being of workers in mind, rather than maximizing profits for absentee shareholders.

The Mondragon Corporation in Spain is one of the most well-known examples of a successful worker cooperative. Mondragon is a federation of cooperatives that spans industries such as manufacturing, retail, and finance. It operates on principles of shared ownership and democratic decision-making, and it has been remarkably resilient through economic crises, in part because its structure aligns the interests of workers and the community. In a post-billionaire economy, this kind of business model would become more prevalent, as it allows wealth to be distributed more fairly among workers and encourages long-term sustainability.

Social Enterprises and Benefit Corporations

Beyond worker ownership, businesses in a post-billionaire economy could be structured as social enterprises or benefit corporations. These are businesses that prioritize social and environmental goals alongside financial performance. Benefit corporations are legally required to consider the impact of their decisions on workers, communities, and the environment, rather than focusing solely on shareholder returns.

In a world without billionaires, companies would be expected to operate under models that balance profit with purpose. For example, a renewable energy company might reinvest its profits into expanding access to clean energy in underserved areas, rather than funneling money into executive bonuses and dividends. Similarly, a tech company could design products with an emphasis on data privacy and ethical technology development, rather than maximizing ad revenue through surveillance capitalism.

These kinds of business models would help ensure that industries are aligned with societal goals, rather than being driven by the relentless pursuit of profit at any cost. By prioritizing workers, communities, and the environment, social enterprises and benefit corporations can contribute to a more equitable and sustainable economy.

Breaking Up Monopolies

In a post-billionaire economy, breaking up monopolies and curbing corporate concentration would be essential to creating a fairer and more competitive marketplace. Today, many industries are dominated by a handful of large corporations—Amazon, Google, Facebook, and Apple, for example—giving these companies immense power over markets, labor conditions, and public policy. Their monopolistic control allows them to extract excessive profits and stifle competition, contributing to the rise of billionaires.

Antitrust regulations would need to be strengthened and rigorously enforced to break up monopolies and prevent corporations from accumulating outsized power. This would not only foster more competition but also encourage innovation and allow smaller, more community-oriented businesses to thrive. Decentralizing economic power in this way would reduce the concentration of wealth and help ensure that the benefits of economic activity are more broadly shared.

4. Emphasizing Sustainability and Long-Term Thinking

One of the most critical aspects of a post-billionaire economy is the emphasis on sustainability and long-term thinking. The current economic model, driven by short-term profits and endless growth, is incompatible with the ecological limits of our planet. A world without billionaires would prioritize environmental sustainability and the responsible management of resources, ensuring that the economy operates within the boundaries of what the Earth can support.

Green Energy and Sustainable Industries

A post-billionaire economy would invest heavily in green energy and sustainable industries. Fossil fuel companies, many of which are owned and controlled by billionaires, would be replaced by renewable energy cooperatives and publicly owned utilities that prioritize clean energy production. These green energy systems would be designed to meet the needs of communities while minimizing environmental impact, rather than being driven by the profit motives of private corporations.

Sustainable industries—such as organic agriculture, circular manufacturing, and regenerative forestry—would become the backbone of the economy. These industries would focus on producing goods and services in ways that minimize waste, reduce carbon emissions, and protect ecosystems. In contrast to today's extractive industries, which prioritize short-term profits at the expense of long-term environmental health, sustainable industries would be guided by principles of ecological stewardship and social responsibility.

Long-Term Investments in Public Goods

In a post-billionaire economy, investment decisions would prioritize long-term societal needs over short-term financial returns. This means that public infrastructure, education, healthcare, and environmental protection would receive sustained investment, even if these sectors do not generate immediate profits. For example, investments in public transit systems, clean water infrastructure, and sustainable housing could significantly reduce carbon emissions and improve quality of life, even if they do not provide quick financial returns for investors.

By focusing on long-term investments in public goods, a post-billionaire economy would be better equipped to address the pressing challenges of climate change, resource depletion, and social inequality. These investments would be designed to benefit future generations, ensuring that the economy is sustainable not just for the next quarter, but for the next century.

5. Strengthening Democratic Institutions

Finally, a post-billionaire economy would be characterized by stronger and more resilient democratic institutions. The outsized influence that billionaires currently have over politics, media, and public policy undermines democratic governance and erodes trust in institutions. Without billionaires, political power would be more evenly distributed, and democratic systems would be better able to represent the interests of ordinary citizens.

Publicly Funded Elections

One of the key reforms in a post-billionaire economy would be the implementation of publicly funded elections. By eliminating private campaign contributions, which allow billionaires to buy political influence, publicly funded elections would ensure that candidates are accountable to the public rather than to wealthy donors. This would help level the playing field and restore trust in democratic processes, allowing for a more representative government.

Media Ownership and Public Information

Another critical reform would be the democratization of media ownership. Today, many media outlets are owned by billionaires, who use their platforms to shape public opinion and advance their personal agendas. In a post-billionaire economy, media ownership would be more decentralized, with a greater emphasis on public media and community-based journalism. This would ensure that the public has access to accurate, unbiased information, free from the influence of wealthy elites.

Envisioning a Fairer, More Sustainable Future

A post-billionaire economy is not an unattainable utopia—it is a realistic alternative to the current system of extreme wealth concentration and inequality. By prioritizing collective well-being, equitable resource distribution, worker-centered businesses, sustainability, and robust democratic institutions, we can create an economy that serves the needs of all people, not just the wealthiest few.

This vision requires bold reforms and a shift in values, but the benefits would be profound. A world without billionaires would be one where poverty and inequality are dramatically reduced, where workers have more control over their lives and livelihoods, where the environment is protected for future generations, and where democracy is strengthened rather than undermined by concentrated wealth.

Building a post-billionaire economy will not happen overnight, but it is a goal worth striving for—a goal that can lead to a more just, equitable, and sustainable world for all.

Chapter 15: The Path Forward

As we reach the culmination of this book, we have explored the moral, economic, social, and environmental consequences of allowing extreme wealth concentration in the hands of a few individuals. Billionaire wealth is not only a symbol of inequality but a driver of systemic imbalances that harm democracy, economic stability, and the planet. We've also examined potential solutions: wealth limits, progressive taxation, corporate reforms, and the redistribution of resources for the collective well-being of society. But while diagnosing the problem and envisioning a more just and equitable future is crucial, the final question remains: How do we get there?

In this final chapter, we map out a comprehensive strategy for moving toward a post-billionaire society. This roadmap will consider actions for governments, corporations, communities, and individuals. It emphasizes the importance of systemic change, grassroots movements, and the power of everyday people to challenge the status quo. While the road ahead is undoubtedly long and difficult, this chapter seeks to inspire hope and determination, showing that change is possible with collective action.

1. Key Reforms: Building a Post-Billionaire Framework

The first and most essential step toward eliminating billionaires is to implement reforms that address the structural causes of wealth accumulation. These reforms will not only aim to redistribute wealth but also to prevent the creation of new billionaires by changing the underlying systems that allow for extreme wealth concentration. Below are the critical reforms necessary to move toward a more equitable society.

Progressive Taxation and Wealth Caps

The most direct way to curb the concentration of wealth is through progressive taxation. Governments must introduce and enforce tax policies that target the top earners, particularly those whose fortunes exceed a certain threshold. These taxes should include:

- **High Marginal Income Taxes:** Taxing the highest earners at significantly higher rates, particularly for incomes above a set level, such as $1 million or more per year.

- **Wealth Taxes:** Taxing accumulated wealth, including property, investments, and other assets, above a certain level. A wealth tax targets wealth that has already been accumulated rather than just income.

- **Capital Gains Taxes:** Ensuring that capital gains (profits from investments) are taxed at the same rates as earned income, closing a loophole that allows the wealthy to pay lower effective tax rates.

- **Inheritance Taxes:** Preventing the concentration of wealth across generations through high inheritance taxes on large estates, ensuring that billionaire fortunes are not passed down intact to heirs, perpetuating inequality.

- **Wealth Caps:** Establishing a wealth ceiling, or maximum allowable personal fortune, beyond which further accumulation is subject to steep taxes or redistribution. This ensures that no individual accumulates more wealth than is reasonable or socially justifiable.

These tax measures would serve not only to redistribute wealth but also to signal that extreme accumulation of resources by a few individuals is no longer acceptable in a fair society. The revenues generated by these taxes can be reinvested into public services, universal basic income, education, healthcare, and infrastructure—ensuring that wealth serves the public good rather than private excess.

Corporate Reforms

Reforming how corporations operate is another key aspect of dismantling the billionaire class. Today, corporate governance structures prioritize shareholder returns, driving companies to maximize short-term profits at the expense of workers, communities, and the environment. To combat this, the following corporate reforms must be implemented:

- **Worker Co-Ownership:** Encouraging or mandating the creation of co-ownership models, where workers own shares in the companies they work for and have a say in management decisions. This ensures that wealth generated by companies is shared more equitably.

- **Corporate Governance Reform:** Mandating that corporate boards include worker representatives and are held accountable to multiple stakeholders (not just shareholders), including employees, communities, and the environment.

- **Anti-Monopoly Regulations:** Strengthening antitrust laws to break up monopolistic corporations, ensuring that no single company or individual has too much control over any given industry or market. Breaking up monopolies would foster competition, innovation, and fairer distribution of profits.

- **Fair Wages and Benefits:** Mandating living wages and comprehensive benefits for all workers, ensuring that the wealth generated by corporations is more equitably distributed among those who contribute to it.

These reforms would democratize wealth creation and distribution within corporations, reducing the disproportionate power that billionaire owners and shareholders hold over the economy and labor markets.

Strengthening Public Services and Social Safety Nets

Redistributing wealth from billionaires is only one part of the solution. The other part involves ensuring that the public has access to high-quality, universal services that reduce the need for individuals to accumulate excessive personal wealth in the first place. These services should include:

- Universal Healthcare: **Providing free or affordable healthcare for all, ensuring that no one has to** accumulate wealth to protect themselves from medical costs.

- **Free Education:** Offering free access to high-quality education from early childhood through higher education, reducing the financial burden on families and empowering individuals with knowledge and skills.

- **Affordable Housing:** Implementing public housing initiatives to ensure that everyone has access to safe and affordable homes, reducing homelessness and the cost of living.

- **Public Transportation:** Expanding and improving public transit systems to reduce dependency on private vehicles, making cities more livable and reducing environmental impact.

- **Universal Basic Income (UBI):** Providing a guaranteed minimum income to all citizens to ensure that everyone can meet their basic needs, regardless of employment status or economic conditions.

By providing universal access to these essential services, society can reduce the need for extreme wealth accumulation, allowing people to live with dignity and security without the pressure to hoard resources.

2. Individual Action: Challenging Billionaire Power

While systemic change is necessary, individuals also play a crucial role in challenging the status quo and pushing for a post-billionaire society. Individual actions can create a ripple effect, raising awareness, influencing public opinion, and pushing policymakers to act. Below are some ways individuals can contribute to the movement for a more equitable future.

Raising Awareness and Changing the Narrative

One of the most important things individuals can do is to challenge the narrative surrounding billionaires and extreme wealth. For too long, the media and society have celebrated billionaires as symbols of success, innovation, and hard work.

By questioning this narrative and raising awareness of the harm caused by wealth concentration, individuals can shift public perception and create momentum for change.

- **Educate Yourself and Others:** Stay informed about the realities of wealth inequality, tax policies, and corporate power. Share this knowledge with your community, friends, and family to challenge common misconceptions.

- **Support Ethical Media:** Seek out and support media outlets that critically examine wealth concentration and billionaire power, rather than glorifying extreme wealth. Social media can be a powerful tool for spreading awareness and sharing alternative perspectives.

- **Confront Wealth Glorification:** Challenge the glorification of billionaires in popular culture. Call out problematic narratives in films, TV shows, and advertisements that portray extreme wealth as desirable or a sign of moral virtue.

Consumer Power and Ethical Choices

Individuals can also use their purchasing power to support businesses that align with the values of a post-billionaire society. This involves being mindful of where your money goes and choosing to support ethical companies, cooperatives, and businesses that prioritize workers, communities, and the environment over profit maximization.

- **Support Worker-Owned Cooperatives:** Whenever possible, choose to buy from cooperatives or worker-owned businesses that share their profits more equitably and prioritize ethical practices.

- Avoid Billionaire-Owned Corporations: Reduce your spending on products and services offered by billionaire-owned corporations that exploit workers, avoid taxes, or engage in harmful environmental practices. This might involve choosing local businesses, shopping secondhand, or buying from socially responsible companies.

- Ethical Investment: If you have investments, consider placing your money in socially responsible investment funds or cooperatives, rather than in large corporations that contribute to wealth concentration.

While individual choices alone cannot dismantle billionaires, collective consumer action can send a powerful message to companies and governments that people are demanding change.

Advocacy and Political Engagement

To truly shift the balance of power away from billionaires, political engagement and advocacy are essential. Individuals must push for systemic change through political channels, demanding that elected officials prioritize policies that curb wealth inequality and support a more equitable society.

- Support Progressive Candidates: Vote for and support candidates who are committed to implementing wealth taxes, corporate reforms, and social safety nets. Grassroots political movements often start with local elections, so engaging at all levels of government is crucial.

- **Join Advocacy Groups:** Join organizations or movements that advocate for wealth redistribution, labor rights, environmental sustainability, and corporate reform. Advocacy groups can amplify individual voices and create coordinated campaigns for change.

- **Push for Campaign Finance Reform:** Advocate for publicly funded elections and campaign finance reform to reduce the influence of billionaires in politics. Supporting efforts to limit political donations from wealthy individuals and corporations can help ensure that democracy is not undermined by private interests.

3. Grassroots Organizing: The Power of Collective Action

While individual action is important, collective action is even more powerful in creating systemic change. Grassroots organizing has historically played a pivotal role in challenging entrenched power structures and advancing social justice. By coming together in movements, unions, and community organizations, people can push for the reforms needed to dismantle billionaire power.

Building Labor Power

One of the most effective ways to challenge the billionaire class is through the power of labor. Historically, unions have been critical in advocating for fair wages, workers' rights, and more equitable distribution of wealth. In a post-billionaire society, strengthening labor power is essential.

- **Join a Union:** If you're a worker, consider joining a union or organizing your workplace. Unions can advocate for better wages, benefits, and working conditions, reducing the wealth gap between workers and owners.

- **Support Workers' Strikes:** When workers strike for fairer treatment, public support is crucial. Whether through financial contributions, participation in solidarity actions, or raising awareness, supporting workers' rights movements can help shift power away from billionaires and corporate owners.

- **Advocate for Labor Rights Legislation:** Push for policies that protect the right to unionize, ensure fair wages, and protect workers from exploitation. Labor-friendly laws can level the playing field between workers and employers, preventing billionaires from hoarding profits at the expense of their workforce.

Grassroots Movements for Wealth Redistribution

Beyond labor, grassroots movements focused on wealth redistribution are crucial to challenging the power of billionaires. These movements often organize around specific policies, such as wealth taxes or universal basic income, and work to build public pressure on policymakers.

- **Organize Locally:** Local grassroots movements can be particularly effective in pushing for change at the municipal or state level, from advocating for local wealth taxes to pushing for affordable housing initiatives.

- **Engage in Direct Action:** Participating in protests, sit-ins, and other forms of direct action can draw attention to the issue of wealth inequality and pressure governments and corporations to act. Many successful social movements have used direct action to bring about significant change.

- **Build Coalitions:** Effective grassroots organizing often involves building coalitions with other groups, including environmentalists, labor unions, civil rights organizations, and community groups. By working together, these coalitions can create broad-based support for wealth redistribution policies.

4. International Cooperation: Addressing Global Wealth Inequality

Wealth inequality is not just a national issue; it is a global one. Billionaires often operate across borders, using tax havens and offshore accounts to avoid paying their fair share. To create a post-billionaire world, international cooperation is essential.

Closing Tax Havens

One of the biggest obstacles to addressing global wealth inequality is the existence of tax havens, where the ultra-wealthy hide their fortunes to avoid paying taxes in their home countries. Governments must work together to close these loopholes and ensure that billionaires cannot evade taxes.

- **Global Tax Transparency:** Countries should push for international agreements that promote tax transparency, requiring corporations and individuals to disclose where their assets are held and how much tax they are paying.

- **Sanctions on Tax Havens:** Countries that allow billionaires to hide their wealth should face sanctions and penalties. By creating consequences for allowing tax evasion, the international community can make it more difficult for billionaires to hoard wealth in offshore accounts.

International Labor Rights and Environmental Standards

Billionaires often exploit weak labor and environmental regulations in developing countries to maximize their profits. To address this, international cooperation is needed to ensure that labor and environmental standards are upheld globally.

- **Global Labor Standards:** International organizations and agreements should set minimum labor standards that all countries must adhere to, preventing billionaires from exploiting workers in countries with weaker protections.

- **Environmental Accountability:** International environmental agreements should hold corporations accountable for their impact on climate change and biodiversity loss, ensuring that billionaires cannot profit from the destruction of the planet.

5. An Optimistic Vision: Change is Possible

As daunting as the task may seem, it's important to remember that change is possible. Throughout history, people have risen up against entrenched power structures and brought about profound social, economic, and political transformations.

Whether through labor movements, civil rights struggles, or environmental activism, ordinary people have shown that they can challenge the status quo and create a more just and equitable world.

The path toward a post-billionaire society will not be easy. It will require courage, determination, and collective action. But the alternative—a world dominated by a small group of ultra-wealthy individuals while millions struggle in poverty and the planet faces ecological collapse—is far worse.

This book has laid out the case against billionaires and provided a roadmap for how we can move toward a more just and equitable future. Now, the responsibility rests with us—with you. Change begins with challenging the systems of inequality that allow billionaires to exist and with building a movement that prioritizes collective well-being over individual wealth.

The path forward is clear: we must push for progressive taxation, corporate reform, universal services, and grassroots organizing. We must challenge the glorification of billionaires, advocate for systemic change, and hold those in power accountable. Together, we can create a world where extreme wealth and inequality are no longer tolerated, and where justice and fairness prevail.

In the words of civil rights leader Martin Luther King Jr., "The arc of the moral universe is long, but it bends toward justice." The path forward is part of that long arc, and with sustained effort, we can bend it toward a future where billionaires are no longer the defining feature of our economic system and where human dignity, fairness, and sustainability are prioritized.

Don't miss out!

Visit the website below and you can sign up to receive emails whenever Jack Donahue publishes a new book. There's no charge and no obligation.

https://books2read.com/r/B-A-WCSZ-XOEAF

BOOKS 2 READ

Connecting independent readers to independent writers.

www.ingramcontent.com/pod-product-compliance
Lightning Source LLC
Chambersburg PA
CBHW071952150726
47999CB00001B/411